Map of the World Shewing the Tracks of the U.S. Exploring Expedition in 1838, 39, 40, 41 & 42

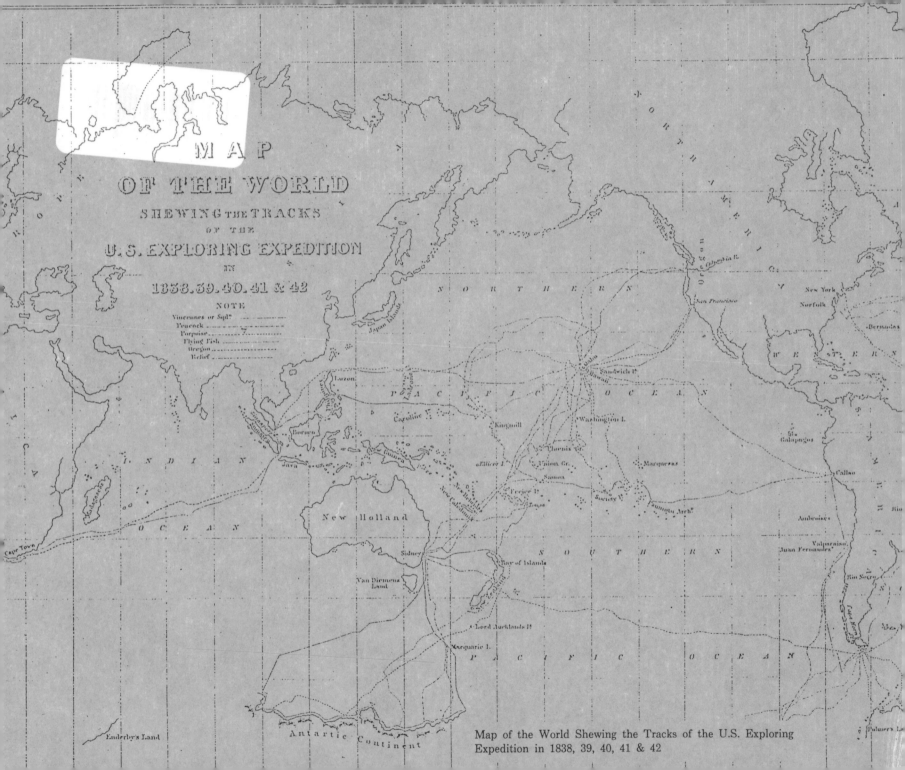

Map of the World Shewing the Tracks of the U.S. Exploring Expedition in 1838, 39, 40, 41 & 42

Map of the World Shewing the Tracks of the U.S. Exploring
Expedition in 1838, 39, 40, 41 & 42

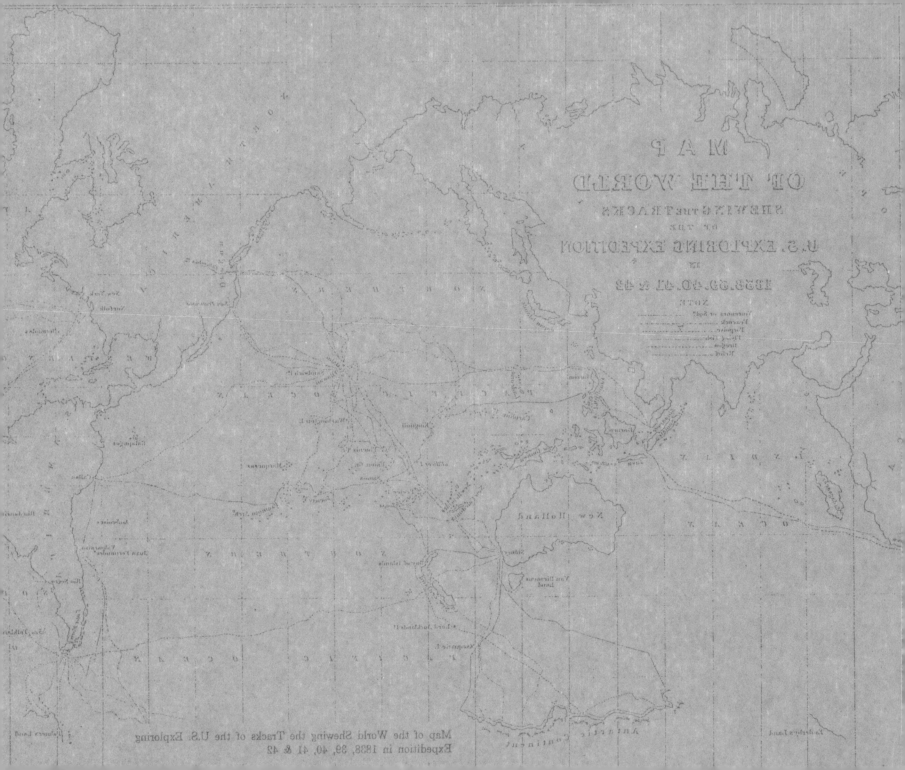

Map of the World Shewing the Tracks of the U.S. Exploring
Expedition in 1838, 39, 40, 41 & 42

THE WILKES EXPEDITION
Puget Sound And The Oregon Country

Frances B. Barkan
Editor

Washington State Capital Museum
Olympia, Washington
1987

Publication Committee

Frances B. Barkan

Drew Crooks, Curator of Collections, Washington State Capital Museum

Les Eldridge, Thurston County Commissioner and Vice Chairman, Maritime Committee, Washington Centennial Commission

Patrick Haskett, Marine Historian

Derek Valley, Director, Washington State Capital Museum

The Publication Committee wishes to sincerely thank

Carl N. Applebaum

The Evergreen State College, Photo Services

Patty M. Maddox, Director, Library and Photographic Services, U.S. Naval Institute

John Norton

The Oregon Historical Society

Margery B. and Ed Owens

Sandra Steffler

Stone McLaren, Design

University of Washington Libraries, Special Collections Division

1989 Washington Centennial Commission

Washington State Historical Society

Washington State Library, Washington Room, Jeanne Engermann and Gayle Palmer

Washington State Printer, Leland Blankenship, State Printer

Representative Joe Williams, Chairman, Maritime Committee, Centennial Commission

To the Memory of Frances B. Barkan

Always looking for a new challenge, Fran was a student of history and life, bringing an inspirational attitude to work and play, she was a delight to know.

The Washington State Capital Museum is publishing this book as part of the Museum's celebration of the Washington Centennial.

TABLE OF CONTENTS

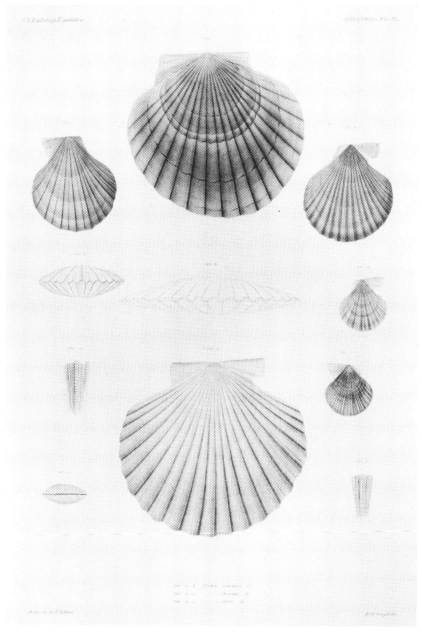

Plate 42, Atlas to Volume XII, *Mollusca and Shells*
(Washington State Library)

PREFACE

The United States Exploring Expedition (1838—1842) was the nation's first maritime attempt to pursue the international pastime of seeking new lands for commercial exploitation, and the wealth and prestige such opportunities would bring to the parent nation. Though Americans had been moving west for almost two centuries, they did not view the move to the Pacific Coast as "colonial." Rather, the western settlement drive, they thought, was an expression of America's right to occupy the entire continent. The western lands were alien, strange to eyes accustomed to the gentler east; the resident Indians, and their societies, were as different from 19th century American city life as could be imagined. Nonetheless, the western expansion was considered normal, a natural move for America to make, and a logical extension of the country's pattern of settlement from the time of the earliest European colonies.

The Wilkes Expedition helped solidify America's interest in "sea to shining sea," and gave policy-makers and ordinary Americans an impression of life in the Oregon Country. In addition, it whetted American appetites for colonies in the South Pacific and other exotic locales. The Expedition provided the stuff dreams are made of—both the dreams of ordinary people looking for escape from their every-day lives, and the dreams of politicians, looking for new projects to cement their appeal to voters. The ships and men were threatened by icebergs around the southern continent, hostile islanders in the South Pacific, and storms all along their route, appealing to Americans' sense of adventure and their desire for excitement.

The Expedition also helped to establish the United States as a great scientific power. With the tens of thousands of specimens the Expedition collected around the globe, a national museum of science was given life, and the contributions of American scientists to the body of scientific knowledge were acknowledged by their colleagues the world over.

However, the Expedition's achievements were almost lost in the intense and bitter wrangling that accompanied the ships' return from sea. Charles Wilkes and some of his officers subjected each other to bitter public attack, raising questions and making accusations about conduct, performance of duty, and, in the long run, integrity and honesty. The new administration, which had been elected while the Expedition was at sea, was largely indifferent to the accomplishments of the nation's first government-sponsored naval exploration. The naval establishment was not particularly receptive, and, for a time, it appeared as if the thousands of boxes of specimens would be scattered to museums and institutions around the country.

Nonetheless, the Expedition's surveys and specimens have tangible value; more than that, they are still significant today. Daniel Henderson, in his 1953 biography of Charles Wilkes, reported that Commander C. Denby Wilkes used his ancestor's charts in the Pacific campaigns of World War II.[1] Materials brought back by the scientists are still housed in the vaults of the Smithsonian, used by researchers and in exhibits. Finally, the Expedition was the nation's first attempt to expand its sphere of influence far beyond its own borders, across the world to Antarctica and Oceania, and across the continent to the far western shore.

Notes on Sources

The writers in this publication have used Charles Wilkes' diary, published in the *Washington Historical Quarterly* in 1925 and 1926. This version was edited by Washington's best-known historian, Edmond S. Meany. In addition, the five-volume *Narrative*, the official publication of the Expedition, was also used. Several editions of this work have been published. Finally, several histories of the Expedition and its work have been published. More details about these works are included in the Bibliography.

In his diary, Wilkes was careless about spelling, punctuation, and grammar; the *Narrative* was polished by an editor prior to publication. Entries from the diary used in this book preserve Wilkes' own constructions. It should be noted that at the time, there was not so distinct an American grammar and language as exists today. Wilkes still used the "our" spelling of words such as "harbor"; in addition, he also used the collective singular, a verb form still common today in the British Isles but not in the United States. For example, Wilkes wrote, "The Company *have*..." An American author today would write "The Company *has*..." Using Wilkes' original language gives some of the flavor of his thoughts.

Three primary sources were used for the list of place names Wilkes gave to Washington and Oregon locales. Edmond S. Meany's classic *Origin of Washington Geographic Names* was first published as a book in 1923; parts of the text were printed in the *Washington Historical Quarterly* earlier. Robert Hitchman's *Place Names of Washington* is a more recent publication. Publications of the Wilkes Expedition were also used.

Notes on Illustrations

Illustrations were prepared by several artists who participated in the Expedition; many of the officers and scientists also made drawings. Published copies of the *Narrative* included many illustrations of places, such as Fort Vancouver, as well as drawings of Indian artifacts and activities such as fishing. Illustrations of scientific specimens were published in atlases, companion volumes to the *Narrative*. In addition, maps and charts made on the voyage were published. Names of these volumes have been included in the bibliography. All charts used in this publication come from the collection of the Washington State Library. Other illustrations were provided by the Oregon Historical Society and the University of Washington Libraries.

Notes on Usages

The sailors' vocabulary is vast and specialized, and uses terms that have no precise equivalent in the common tongue. It is not surprising that sailors, isolated from land for months or years at a time, should develop a special language to describe their circumstances, their physical surroundings, and their companions. Even in modern times, the sailors' language has persisted, and captains of the smallest pleasure boats use terms that have their origins in the great age of sail.

Jack tar (abbreviated to *Jack*) was a commonly-used nickname for sailors. It is said to derive from the tarred canvas seamen wore in bad weather. The term Jack appears in sailor's songs and poetry, and was used by officers to refer to their men.

Passed midshipman was a rank used in the U. S. Navy during the 19th century. The peace-time Navy had too many higher ranking officers, and too many midshipmen looking for—and deserving of—promotion. Midshipmen entered the Navy at about age 14, and served at this rank for about three years. As soon as they passed an examination on navigation and seamanship, they received the rank of "Passed Midshipman," and their pay was boosted from $400 to $750 per year.[2] Passed midshipmen were watch-keeping officers, and often performed all the duties of a lieutenant.

Ships of the time were rigged in every conceivable way, in order to best take advantage of wind and sea conditions. An encyclopedia of ship rigs of the 19th century would show, most commonly, two or three masts, and a combination of *square* and *fore-and-aft* sails. *Square* sails are usually rectangular in shape, and are set on a *yard* (a spar placed across the mast to hold sails) athwartships. *Fore-and-aft* sails are three or four-cornered, and are set along the fore-and-aft line of the hull (most modern sailboats are fore-and-aft rigged). A 19th century ship might be entirely fore-and-aft or square-rigged, but more than likely had a combination of these sail types to ensure a good turn of speed under a variety of conditions.

A *brig*, such as the Expedition's *Porpoise*, had two masts, and was usually square-rigged on both masts. Modifications of this type included the *hermaphrodite* and *jackass* brigs, which were square-rigged on the foremast and fore-and-aft rigged on the main mast. *Porpoise* had originally been rigged as a *brigantine*, a ship with two masts which had both fore-and-aft and square sails on the mainmast. In the twentieth century, the term brigantine has come to mean a two-masted vessel, square-rigged on the foremast and fore-and-aft rigged on the mainmast.

A *frigate* was a three-masted, *ship-rigged* vessel—that is, she was square-rigged on all three masts.

A *schooner*, such as the *Flying Fish*, was fore-and-aft rigged on all masts; the shortest mast is the foremost one, while the largest is furthest aft. The largest schooners had seven masts. The schooner design is still used for some pleasure boats, though modern schooners are usually two-masted.

A *ship*, technically speaking, was any vessel with three (or more) square-rigged masts. However, sailors used the term to mean any vessel.

A *sloop-of-war*, such as *Vincennes*, was ship-rigged, but was smaller than a frigate. Usually, a frigate carried between 24 and 50 guns on one or two gun-decks. A sloop-of-war, sometimes referred to as a *ship-sloop*, carried between 18 and 32 guns on one deck.

Porpoise and Schooner Separating

Frances B. Barkan

(Les Eldridge contributed to this chapter)

Charles Wilkes, Commander, USN

CHARLES WILKES— LIEUTENANT COMMODORE

by

Frances B. Barkan

Charles Wilkes' life was neatly circumscribed by the Great Exploring Expedition, though the actual voyage occupied only four years of his long naval career. Nearly two years were devoted to planning and preparation for the journey, and the writing of the *Narrative* and its accompanying publications kept Wilkes occupied for years afterwards. Furthermore, the controversies surrounding both his appointment as commander, and the return of the Expedition to the U.S., cast a deep shadow over the rest of his naval service. Despite his role as commander of the first U.S. government-sponsored nautical exploration, and his heroism in the Civil War, discord followed him throughout his life, leading to court martial, accusations of insubordination, and a forced retirement from the service. He was marked as a black sheep—and apparently felt compelled to reinforce that image at every chance.

In many ways, Wilkes was the ideal sailor to lead the Expedition on its odyssey. He was highly skilled in navigation and surveying, fascinated by the intricacies of these arts. His chartwork was accurate, and he was diligent in supervising the survey work of his officers, checking discrepancies, and eliminating the effects of fancy and laziness.

On the other hand, Wilkes was far from an ideal commander. He was temperamental, easily angered, and, some of his critics said, too quick to punish his crew members for minor infractions. Wilkes was no diplomat, and his own words show him to be judgmental about others, perhaps holding up too high a standard of behavior or dress to make a fair assessment of character. Wilkes was a formal man, who valued propriety (perhaps excessively); he was used to having things his own way. He was apparently unable to keep silent about his feelings. A little tact might have produced the results he desired, or could have created a more receptive climate for his ideas and actions. Instead, his colleagues were more often offended at his choice of words and his manner, giving them reasons—or excuses—to ignore Wilkes' talents, skills, and very real discoveries. The picture that emerges is that of a difficult, stiff-necked, rebellious man with a streak of self-destructiveness. One cannot but wonder how much further such fine talents might have taken a more personable officer.

Unfortunately, Wilkes' lack of leadership ability was exacerbated by the reluctance of the Federal government to grant him an appropriate commander's rank—a loss which he felt keenly. His request for a captaincy was refused, and Wilkes led the Expedition as a lieutenant—the same rank as the other ships' commanders. Wilkes was clearly appointed expedition leader, but his lack of appropriate rank was to cause serious problems. In the Navy, as in other military services, rank—and the privileges and responsibilities that go with it—are of utmost importance, equal in value to knowledge and skills in the military arts. Wilkes, at the time the Expedition left on its four-year journey, was not only a mere lieutenant, but a junior lieutenant, with less seniority than many of his colleagues. The naval officers who served in the Expedition were well aware of this situation, and some resented deeply the attitudes and privileges of command Wilkes arrogated to himself. Wilkes, on the other hand, felt that his responsibilities as Expedition leader allowed him to take the trappings of rank. He and Lieutenant Hudson, master of the *Peacock*, came to a remarkable agreement that both would wear captain's uniforms, and try to conceal from the rest of the crew the denial by the Navy of their appointments to that rank.[1]

Early Service

Wilkes was born in New York, to well-off parents of English, Scottish, and French ancestry. His father, who emigrated to America as a young man, came from a wealthy English family. The elder Wilkes was not sympathetic to the American revolution, and left the colonies during the war of independence. Nevertheless, after the war ended, he returned to New York, married, and raised his family. The young Wilkes requested that his father find him a midshipman's berth in the Navy and, with some reluctance, the father agreed. Wilkes served in the merchant marine on the advice of the Secretary of the Navy, to gain sea time while he was waiting for his midshipman's appointment, and returned home with a great fund of practical experience in navigation.

After service in the Mediterranean and in South America, Wilkes was appointed head of the Navy's Depot of Charts and Instruments. In 1836, he eagerly carried out a commission to travel to Europe to purchase instruments for the Expedition, which had been in the planning stages for a number of years.

The United States Exploring Expedition

Wilkes had already been considered for command of a vessel in the United States Exploring Expedition, which was to be headed by Captain Thomas ap Catesby Jones. Under this plan, Wilkes would be in charge of nautical science, and be responsible for scientific instruments and surveying. However, Wilkes could not bring himself to accept a minor role, and requested that his name be withdrawn from consideration.

In 1837, the Secretary of War, recognizing Wilkes' knowledge of navigation, astronomy, magnetism, and hydrography and geodetics, asked him to lead the Expedition. Wilkes was chosen over higher-ranking officers, and his appointment also bypassed many Navy lieutenants who were technically senior to him. Though these officers may not have wanted the job, and though Wilkes' superior skills made him a logical choice, his appointment left considerable bitterness in certain quarters.

The Expedition was already controversial when Wilkes' appointment was made. It had taken years to get the voyage approved, funded, and prepared. The Expedition would bring prestige to the new nation, laying the foundation for an empire that would permit the United States to stand equal in stature and wealth with its older European colleagues, some said. Others thought the idea a complete waste of money. In many ways, the conflicts over the proposed voyage were similar to today's disputes concerning the worth of the space program. The selection of a commander under these circumstances fueled a smoldering fire, and the appointment of a junior lieutenant, no matter how talented, raised eyebrows in both political and naval establishments.

The strains of a four-year voyage, away from home, family, and familiar surroundings, created conditions that led even the most mild-tempered to exasperation, frustration, and hatred. Wilkes' personality, and his lack of an appropriate commander's rank, led to bitter clashes with the other ranking officers. Though they admired his abilities as a surveyor, the lieutenants serving under Wilkes found him to be exacting and sometimes petty. Even those who managed to work well with Wilkes found themselves on the punishment roster, and minor incidents led to major explosions. Wilkes expected to be obeyed, treated in a manner appropriate to his station even if his rank did not ensure him the deference of his officers. Furthermore, he presumed that the work of the Expedition would be accomplished as he chose. His expectations were thwarted, at least in his own mind, and he exercised what he felt was his right as commander to punish the offenders.

As the ships entered the Strait of Juan de Fuca on May 1, he suspended Lieutenant Thomas Budd for "persisting to (exercise) studding sails whilst torn."[2] On May 9, Lieutenant James Alden was suspended for "not having made his appearance on the forecastle when the topsails were sheeting home" and for having, in the process, "stood several calls" (not responding to the boatswain's call to appear on deck).[3] On July 17th, Lieutenant Robert Johnson (whose name Wilkes often spelled "Johnstone"), prompted the following diary entry

"I returned yesterday from a surveying excursion with the boats and agreeably to orders found everything ready for sailing. embarked the remainder of the Instruments &c. &c. and prepared for departure. A 2 P.M. the wind sprang up from the westward hove up the anchor and made sail. Lt. Johnstone had been prepared with Pas^d Mid. Eld to cross over to the Chikeles [Chehalis] River for the purpose of proceeding down it, to its mouth in Gray's Harbour, and making a survey of it, and the Coast as far as the Columbia River including Shoalwater Bay. on the receipt of his written orders, he came to me to expostulate on them in apparent temper. I refused to have anything to say to him. This was on the Quarter Deck whilst heaving up. I told him not to come and speak to me in that mood & told him to go below, and think over what he was about, and to be ready to leave the ship in 5 minutes, that I was anxious to save the tide, & wished him to take his departure immediately, in about 10 minutes he came to me again, & I would not listen to him. He was dressed as I considered very unofficerlike, having on one of the caps, or hat worn by the Indians, and showed marked disrespect in his manner, & dress to the rules of the ship & navy. On his going below in 5 minutes I ordered Lt. Carr 1st Lt. to send a message for Lt. J. to leave the ship immediately finding the time had expired. I again sent Mr. Colvocoresses to tell Mr J. that he must positively leave the Ship in five minutes and after the expiration of this time Lt. J. came on deck, came to me in some temper & in this dress before described with my written orders in his hand, and on my telling him he must positively leave the ship under those orders, he said he would not obey the orders or words to that effect, and thereupon I took the orders from his hand, he at the time said he wished to keep them, but this I refused and immediately suspended him from duty"[4]

Wilkes accused some officers of creating a "cabal" and plotting against him; he was especially suspicious of Thomas Craven and Samuel P. Lee, both of whom had been originally under the command of Captain Thomas ap Catesby Jones. These "dissidents" were sent home, released from their Expedition duties. Other officers received tongue-lashings and the brunt of Wilkes' dislike. The Expedition's members were able to pull together and work effectively, but it could not be said, when the Expedition arrived home, that Wilkes had made friends.

Wilkes may have been wrong about the cabal, but a look at Craven's and Lee's later careers gives some indication that Wilkes may have been right about their abilities and dedication to duty. Craven, suspended from duty in Tierra del Fuego when he failed to carry on any surveying while Lieutenant Ringgold, his commander, was ashore, was sent home aboard the *Relief* from Callao.[5] Years later, in 1865, Craven commanded a squadron of Union warships (*Niagara* and *Sacramento*) in pursuit of the Confederate ironclad *Stonewall* off the Spanish and Portuguese coasts. Captain Page, her commander, was amazed at Craven's avoidance of pursuit of his quarry off Ferrol and Coruna, and wrote

"But how Captain Craven can excuse himself for not meeting her [*Stonewall*] yesterday, I cannot conceive...his commission would not be worth much in most navies."

Craven later tried to follow *Stonewall* out of Lisbon Harbor without giving her the 24-hour start required by international convention. The Portuguese fired on *Niagara*, and Craven lost nine days, rather than one, before being able to resume pursuit.[6]

Samuel P. Lee was suspended for disrespect to Lieutenant Hudson, and left the Expedition at Valparaiso by mutual consent. Mid-1862 found Lee in command of a Union squadron on the Mississippi under David G. Farragut. Sent to reconnoiter Vicksburg, he instead "fired at and alerted" the Confederate defenders. He then demanded their surrender without devising a plan for attack if the surrender offer was rejected. The Vicksburg defenders refused to surrender, and the squadron ignominiously retired. Lee's subsequent Civil War career was undistinguished. In 1865, Lee was relieved of another command and replaced by a less "conservative" commander.

Interestingly, Craven and Lee, along with Wilkes, were promoted to flag rank during their naval service. The conflicts between them were caused as much by style as anything.

The Return Home

The successes of the voyage could not sever the skeins of controversy which entangled Wilkes and the Expedition members when they returned home. No bands played when the flagship arrived in the port of New York, and Congress failed to pass a resolution of thanks. This was a major blow to the prestige of the Expedition and its commander. President Tyler, who had been inaugurated during the Expedition's absence, seemed indifferent to the return of the ships and the men who had added riches to the growing American empire. Wilkes recorded that the Secretary of the Navy, Abel Upshur, was cold and hostile. Vitriolic accusations and counter-accusations were made by Wilkes and by some of his officers, with the result that Wilkes and the officers were tried on charges ranging from insubordination to giving away public property. Wilkes himself, although indicted for oppression, cruelty, disobedience to orders, scandalous conduct, and illegal punishment of seamen, was found guilty of only the last of these charges, and was publicly reprimanded. Though some viewed this as a mild punishment, Wilkes was infuriated by what he viewed as a major humiliation; he ended his service as leader of the first U.S. exploring voyage under a dark cloud.

The Narrative

Something had to be done with the specimens gathered by the Expedition's scientists, and with the wealth of written material that was to be edited into the Expedition's narrative. Wilkes was determined to write the Expedition's story himself, and he recognized the need to properly preserve the specimens for further study. Wilkes jealously guarded the Expedition's written records, to ensure that the publications emerging from the voyage would reflect his own views.

In addition, the boxes of specimens had to be sorted and appropriately cared for. The first shipment was sent to the Peale Museum in Philadelphia, but after a year that shipment and all other specimens were transferred to the National Institute, the fledgling national museum in Washington, D.C. One of the Expedition's scientists, Charles Pickering, became the initial curator, but after his departure, Wilkes was appointed to supervise the collections. In the Great Hall of the Patent Office, Wilkes established an exhibit of the Expedition's trophies; living plants were sent to the nation's Botanical Gardens. Wilkes was able to command the assistance of some of his former crew members, who started work on the extensive collection of charts. Wilkes himself wrote steadily on the narrative of the Expedition. With the ships' logs and journals written by the officers, Wilkes was able to write the Expedition's story. Illustrations for the *Narrative* were prepared by Joseph Drayton, some from Wilkes' own sketches.

By January, 1844, the five-volume *Narrative* was complete. Congress had approved the printing of 100 copies of the publication, but the contract with the publisher called for a minimum of 250 copies to be printed. Wilkes was given permission to purchase the 150 extra copies, and was further permitted to print his own edition of the *Narrative*, at his expense. However, these seemingly irregular actions once again put him under suspicion of self-enrichment, and he was investigated by a special committee of the Congress. Nothing came of the charges, but it was another thorn in Wilkes' side.

The *Narrative* was reprinted twice, and the publication sold well, to Wilkes' great satisfaction. However, the officers who accompanied Wilkes were not so pleased with the results. Thirteen of them presented a petition to Congress requesting that certain critical remarks be expunged from the next edition of the *Narrative*. Wilkes was again on the defensive.

Wilkes did not return to active duty in the Navy for some years. He requested a command in the war with Mexico in 1846, but received no appointment. He was finally promoted to captain's rank in 1855. This came as part of the Navy's normal promotion of officers, and not because of his unique service as leader of the Expedition. To all intents and purposes, the Navy ignored Wilkes' Expedition achievements.

The Civil War Years

Wilkes waited out the years between the return of the Expedition and the Civil War, working on publications and defending his character from assaults from many quarters. He and his family were socially prominent in Washington, D. C., and he was a regular visitor to the White House. When Lincoln was elected, Wilkes became an intimate of the first Republican president.

In the first year of the Civil War, Wilkes suggested to Secretary of State William Seward that Confederate naval ports be blockaded. The President approved of the plan, and Wilkes was assigned to bring home a needed Federal warship, the screw-sloop *San Jacinto*, from the African coast to join in the hunt for a Confederate raider. During the pursuit, Wilkes learned that a British mail steamer, the *Trent*, was scheduled to sail from Havana to England, carrying Confederate officials bearing dispatches. Wilkes decided to stop the British ship, board her, and take off her Confederate passengers. He carried out the plan, seizing the vessel and taking the Confederates prisoner.

Wilkes found himself a hero, welcomed by parades, speeches, and feasts. However, the President found himself in a dilemma. He could not approve of the seizure of a neutral ship, particularly at a time when British intervention on the side of the South posed a constant threat, but Wilkes' actions were wildly popular. Something had to be done with the prisoners, and the British had requested an apology. A compromise solution was reached, in that the Confederates were released and placed on board a British vessel. Wilkes once again felt snubbed, his decisive action watered down by political squabbling.

Wilkes proposed other ideas to Lincoln and Seward, including the stationing of flotillas to protect the vulnerable Potomac, and a scheme to capture Richmond, Virginia, the Confederate capital, by naval bombardment. At the siege of Richmond, Wilkes, now a commodore, worked hand-in-hand with the Union army commander, General George McClellan. When frustrated Union forces were withdrawn from Richmond, the

Secretary of the Navy appointed Wilkes to the command of a flying squadron in the West Indies which would seek and destroy Confederate privateers.

Under orders from the Secretary of the Navy, Wilkes pursued an extremely successful Confederate raider, the *Alabama*. In order to augment his squadron, which he felt was inadequate for the task, Wilkes simply commandeered two vessels from another American squadron in the Gulf of Mexico, as well as a war steamer, the *Vanderbilt*, which had been despatched on a separate mission to locate the *Alabama*. While looking for the *Alabama*, Wilkes took it upon himself to pursue and capture British ships carrying mail and supplies for the Confederacy, once again creating diplomatic havoc. The British were strong supporters of the cotton-producing southern states, and Confederate supply ships were welcomed in British West Indies ports. The flying squadron used neutral ports, such as Havana, as bases of operation, and seized British ships both on the high seas and in neutral harbors.

Diplomats of the neutral nations, such as Denmark and Spain, as well as Great Britain, of course, were driven to strong protest. The British threatened war with the United States, and Wilkes was relieved of his command in the Caribbean.

The Court Martial

Wilkes was publicly blamed by the Secretary of the Navy for the so far unsuccessful hunt for the *Alabama* and her consorts. In return, Wilkes wrote a stiff letter of protest, which he not only sent to the Secretary but apparently submitted to leading newspapers. The Secretary of the Navy found this action a violation of naval regulations, and called a court of inquiry to determine how the letter was obtained by the press. When the court was unable to find any details about the letter, the Secretary organized a court martial.

Wilkes was charged with disobedience of lawful orders, insubordinate conduct, disrespect and disrespectful language to a superior officer, refusal of obedience to a lawful general order issued by the Secretary of the Navy, and conduct unbecoming an officer. Initially, Wilkes loudly accused the Secretary of the Navy of packing the court, and of preferring the charges out of personal spite. Nevertheless, the court martial proceeded. Wilkes was found guilty on all charges, and suspended for three years from his naval duties. President Lincoln, in his review of the action, declined to approve the sentence, and canceled the charges and the verdict. But the damage had been done—the House of Representatives published the proceedings of the court martial, making this final humiliation public and effectively ending Wilkes' naval career in disgrace.

The Last Years

Wilkes returned to publishing the reports of the Exploring Expedition, now a twenty-five-year-old memory. Three volumes of the original series remained to be finished, including volumes of hydrography, physics, and botany. By 1872, funding for further publications had run out, and Congress was not disposed to grant any additional money for the project. Thus Wilkes' lifework, the results of his greatest effort, was ended. He died in relative obscurity in 1877. Perhaps the greatest irony was that the Exploring Expedition, Wilkes' great obsession, was not mentioned in his obituary.

In The Final Analysis...

Charles Wilkes was a man to be both envied and pitied. He experienced both great success and great failure. His stubbornness and pride made him a good commander but a poor leader of men. His supreme achievement, the successful completion of the first United States exploration, was marred by quarrels on the voyage, and accusations and a court martial when he returned home. His heroism in the Civil War gained him enormous prestige with the public and the opprobrium of the military establishment. He ended his career in disgrace, able to salvage from the wreckage only a few shreds of recognition for his achievements.

There is no doubt that Wilkes was a difficult man. His own writings show him to be rigid, judgmental, and unyielding.[7] Others, writing about him, complain of his arrogance, willful disobedience to orders, and petty diatribes. However, the severe shortcomings of Wilkes' personality can in no way diminish his achievements as leader of the United States Exploring Expedition. Though the journey was fraught with difficulties, and beset by continual dissension among the officers, Wilkes successfully led his ships around the world, charting, surveying, and collecting specimens. He brought back a wealth of information and new ideas, and helped to change the way Americans viewed their nation—not as a little collection of struggling states, but as the progenitor of a vast empire, stretching from coast to coast and around the world. Wilkes helped immeasurably to promote the addition of the West Coast states to the nation.

In the last analysis, Wilkes' personality kept him from achieving recognition of his talents, skills, and accomplishments. He is not well or fondly remembered, as are other great explorers or naval officers, as a lovable eccentric or personable hero. Nonetheless, he should be remembered as one of the Americans who shaped our nation as not only a great world power, occupying the width of the North American continent, but also as a leader in scientific research.

(Les Eldridge contributed to this chapter)

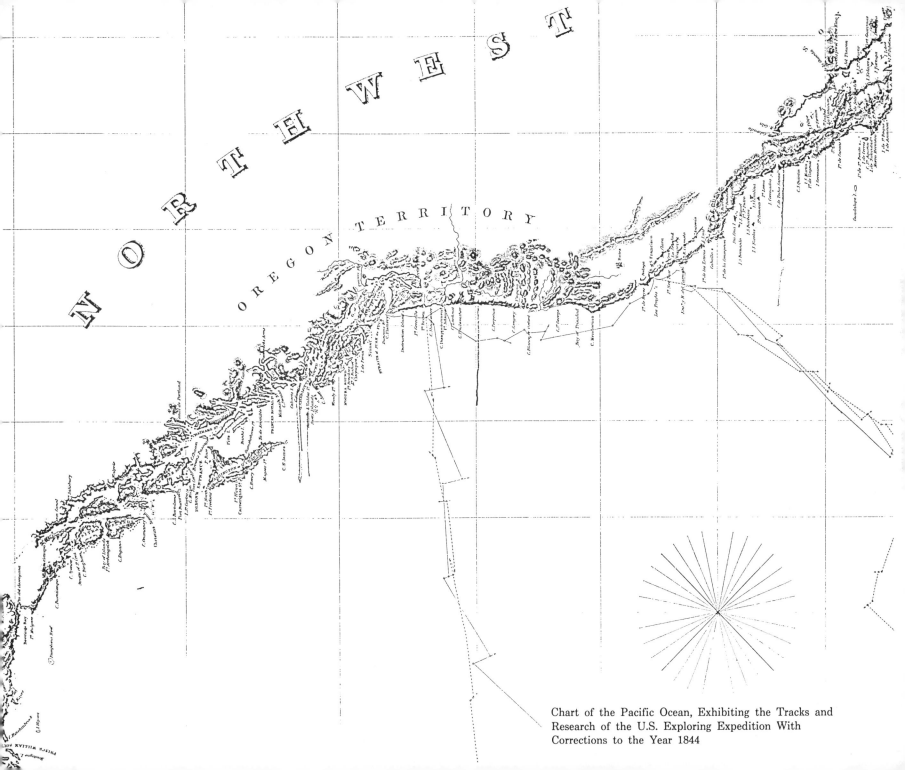

Chart of the Pacific Ocean, Exhibiting the Tracks and
Research of the U.S. Exploring Expedition With
Corrections to the Year 1844

THE LURE OF THE PACIFIC, THE CONTEST OF NATIONS

by

Les Eldridge

The United States Exploring
Expedition of 1838—1842 was the
most ambitious in a series of such
ventures over three-quarters of a century and
involving five nations. It was a major thread
in a tapestry of empire, commerce,
exploration, settlement, and conflict.

The Pacific Northwest was a footnote of
Pacific exploration for many of the
expeditions which preceded Wilkes, and
indeed for Wilkes himself, as the vast scope
of his four-year voyage included Antarctica
and the South Pacific. The Northwest,
literally a far corner of the world, had been
traversed and seen by only a few
adventuresome Europeans during the 16th
through the early 19th century.

Early Explorations of the Northwest Coast

Motives varied greatly
among the Spanish,
French, English,
Russian, and American
explorers and traders
who found their way
to this remote coast.
Some followed dreams
of fortune; others
pursued corporate profits, imperial expansion,
scientific fame, or the discovery of the fabled
Northwest Passage. Behind all these front-
line adventurers were men and women of
great vision and organization talent,
determination, and strength, who sent their
ships and men to the Northwest with the
technological and logistical preparation to
court success if fortune permitted.

The first contact with our Northwest coast
probably occurred 412 years ago when
Francis Drake (as yet unknighted) and the
Golden Hinde made a landfall on the west
coast of North America and turned right
instead of left, missing the Strait of Juan de

Fuca. Two accounts of Drake's voyage place his landfall at 43 degrees north (about the latitude of present-day Coos Bay, Oregon); two others speculate a more northerly landfall at 48 degrees (near Cape Flattery). A 10 day sail took Drake to what is now known as Drake's Bay, California, and his ship's calculated average speed of two knots thus places Drake's landfall at Cape Flattery, rather than further south on the Oregon coast. Many believe Drake searched for the fabled Straits of Anian, looking for a shorter route from Europe to the Indies.

He was followed in 1592 by Apostolos Valerionos de Cephalonia, better known to the Northwest as Juan de Fuca. De Fuca alleged that, in his sailing in the service of Spain, that he had found a large strait between 47 and 48 degrees. He mentioned this discovery several years later in Venice to Michael Lok, a London broker who financed explorations during the era of Elizabeth I. Lok passed it along to Samuel Purchas, a compiler of travel books, who included it in his *Hakluyts' Voyages*.[1] Two hundred years later Charles Barkley of the British East India Company discovered a strait at 48 degrees and a bit, and named the strait for de Fuca.[2]

The first Russian appearance of lasting importance was Bering's 1741 exploration of the Aleutians and the Alaskan coast. For two hundred years, Russian explorers strengthened and defended the Russian fur trade on the Northwest coast. A major effort by Krusenstern and Lisianskii in 1803—1806 attempted to repulse Indian efforts to displace Russian settlers, and had the additional purpose of opening trade opportunities with Japan.

However, a Russian presence was never felt strongly in Puget Sound waters. The first

European exploration of the inland waters that can be documented was Spanish. From San Blas, the west coast naval center of the Vice-Royalty of New Spain, Viceroy Antonio Bucareli sent Juan Perez and Bruno Heceta north in 1774 and 1775. Perez discovered Nootka Sound, on the west coast of Vancouver Island, and, a year later, with Juan Francisco de la Bodega y Quadra, took possession for Spain. Nootka eventually became the chief Spanish post in the Northwest. Heceta noticed the outflow of the Columbia in the same year, and was moved to suspect the existence of the river. From then until about 1790, Bucareli and later Revilla Gigedo sent a flotilla of explorers and cartographers to the British Columbian and Alaskan coasts. Between 1789 and 1794, Alejandro Malaspina surveyed the Pacific coasts of North and South America in an effort to equal the prestige of Cook's voyages and to discover the Northwest Passage.[3] The Napoleonic Wars, England's dispute with Spain over Nootka, and the decay of the Spanish court and government served to remove the Spanish from the Northwest in all but the place names they left behind.

England's next Northwest presence (after Drake's uncertain landfall) was her proudest: Captain James Cook on his last voyage. Cook, a self-taught navigator, was the standard by which other nations judged their explorers; precise, technically brilliant, unflappable, indefatigable. Like many great leaders he taught his craft and inspired accomplishment in those who served with him, including George Vancouver and William Bligh. Cook, like Drake and Malaspina, searched for the Northwest Passage. He arrived on the Oregon coast on March 7, 1778, from his most recent discovery, the Hawaiian Islands.[4] Cook named this archipelago for the fourth Earl of

Sandwich for his patron and First Lord of the Admiralty. Cook named his landfall "New Albion" after Drake's phrase for the same coast, and turned north, only to demonstrate that even the great can err. Off the entrance, and just out of sight of the very passage for which he searched, he entered in his journal

"It is in this very latitude where we now were, that geographers have placed the pretended strait of Juan de Fuca. But we saw nothing like it; not is there the least probability that ever any such thing existed."[5]

His midshipman, George Vancouver, would return twelve years later to explore the strait to its end. Cook proceeded north to Nootka Sound, establishing Britain's claim to the coast, and charted the southern waters of Alaska.

Vancouver's return in 1792 with *HMS Discovery* and *HMS Chatham* left the first, palpable British imprint on what is now western Washington. Exceptionally fine charts of Puget's Sound, south of Elliott Bay (surveyed by Lieutenant Peter Puget and Master Joseph Whidbey), and English place names on prominent features (Mt. Rainier, Mount Baker, Vashon Island) laid a base for subsequent occupation by the Hudson's Bay Company. Typical of the interaction of competing nations in the region was the cooperation between British and Spanish vessels, and the subsequent professional regard that developed between Vancouver and Bodega y Quadra.

The French expedition of de La Perouse in the *Astrolabe* and *Boussole* in 1785—1788 adds a poignant note to the contest of expansion and scientific and cartographic one-up-manship. Inspired by that surveying paragon, Cook, the government of Louis XVI sent Jean Francois Galaup de La Perouse to chart the parts of the Pacific untouched by Cook's three voyages. Charting parts of the Alaskan and British Columbian coasts, de La Perouse, like many before him, missed the Strait of Juan de Fuca in the fog, having named Alaska's Port des Francois. He sailed on to Australia, leaving in his wake French Frigate Shoals (Hawaii) and La Perouse Strait (Japan). The expedition was never heard from after leaving Australia. The wrecks of its ships were discovered on the island of Vanikoro (part of the Solomon Islands chain) more than 38 years later by an itinerant Irish trader, Peter Dillon, after the republican government of France had given up its diligent, but hopeless search for its royalist squadron.[6]

De La Perouse had engaged two astronomers, and in doing so, rejected the application of a young Corsican artillerist and surveyor, Napoleon Buonoparte. The expedition was further distinguished by its visits to "nations, reputedly barbarous, without shedding a drop of blood."[7]

The nations which disclosed the wild Northwest coast to the European consciousness are remembered in the place names along the shore: Fidalgo, Decatur, Rainier, Menzies, Baranof, Prince Rupert, Port des Francois. Interspersed with the European names are centuries-old native locations: Duwamish, Alki Point, Nootka, and Neah Bay. The mix of names was accomplished through a remarkable "sorting out" process which took place after many features had been given two or three names. Captain Henry Kellett of the Royal Navy surveyed the Sound in 1847. In an even-handed example of British fair play at its best, Kellett kept American, British, Spanish, and Indian names in balance and left an international mix.[8] Other surveyors followed, notably James Alden in the steamer *Active* in 1855—1857, who had first served as a lieutenant aboard the *Vincennes* under Wilkes in 1841. Wilkes' record of almost 300 names, however, was never equaled.

The Fur Trade

Cook's voyages, the acme of cartographic excellence, also opened the gates to commerce, for Cook had noted the opportunities for fur trading.

"There is not the least doubt that a very beneficial fur trade might be carried on with the inhabitants of this vast coast."[9]

The first trader reached Nootka in 1785 (a year after the publication of Cook's third voyage saga). Over the years, American and British traders discovered, in their zeal for pelts, the Strait of Juan de Fuca (Charles Barkley, 1787), and the Columbia River (Robert Gray, 1792). The Hudson's Bay Company built the first establishments within present-day Washington state borders during the first years of the 19th century.

The early traders often traversed the Pacific between China and the Northwest coast several times (over a period of years) before returning to the northeastern United States or England. One such navigator was a bravo named John Meares, aboard the *Felice* in 1788. He sailed in company with Charles Barkley, and so was well aware that Barkley had discovered the Strait of Juan de Fuca a year earlier. Yet Meares, in his journal, claims not only discovery, but sets the width of the Strait at twice its actual.[10]

Meares was icebound in Prince William Sound (in modern-day Alaska) in the winter of 1786—1787; it was a prison for Meares'

ship, the *Nootka*, awaiting a rendezvous with the *Sea Otter*.[11] Almost all the crew was lost to scurvy. Meares and his remaining crew were rescued by two of his rivals, Nathaniel Portlock and George Dixon, both East India Company captains. As a condition of their rescue effort, these two trading adversaries forced Meares to agree to stop his activities in the Northwest. Meares had little choice in the matter, and left the Northwest for China.

The next year, Meares developed a scheme to return to the Northwest, and sailed from Macao under the Portuguese flag. As one historian noted, "Meares was no believer in wasting money, and in this category he included the obtaining of proper licenses from the East India Company and the South Sea Company. Accordingly, he took into partnership a Portuguese merchant from Macao."[12] It is clear that Meares was a man to be in the thick of things, undaunted by adversity.

Two years later, at the center of a controversy surrounding claim and counter-claim between Spain and England over Nootka, Meares' return was to cause a war of words between Spain and England, and ultimately gave the British dominion over the Northwest coast. The Spanish, nervous about their rights, seized Meares, his ship, and crew members when Meares appeared to be establishing a colony near the Spanish fort at Nootka. Meares' penchant for exaggeration would inflame Parliament into a hard position on the rights of the King's subjects in the North Pacific. In the resultant "Nootka Convention," Spain acknowledged British rights at Nootka and paid reparation to Meares and his brother captains for the capture of their ships.

The Hudson's Bay Company was the last active pretender to the prize of the Puget

Sound country. Fort Victoria, Fort Nisqually, Fort Vancouver, and Fort George (Astoria) were trading bastions of this remarkably durable commercial empire. The Hudson's Bay Company endured in the Northwest long past the Treaty of 1846, in which Britain abandoned all claim to Oregon territory south of the 49th parallel. The Company endured because of its practice of combining profitable venture with peaceful coexistence. So taken with their hospitality was Wilkes that he named three islands for their employees, including McNeil for Captain William H. McNeill (note Wilkes' consistency in spelling: always incorrect), captain of the steamer *Beaver*, the first steamship in the North Pacific.[13]

The HBC's interest in the Northwest was older than many national claims on the lands and waters of the coast, as the Company had played a part in the search for the Northwest Passage since the establishment of York Fort on Hudson's Bay centuries before. Samuel Hearne had set out from Prince of Wales Fort in 1770 to explore the Northwest Territories and find a northwest passage, if one existed. Hearne learned to live like the Chipewayans, who befriended him, and successfully returned to the Bay 19 months after leaving. He reached the Arctic Ocean at the mouth of the Coppermine River. "There was no Northwest Passage; it was a rocky suburb of Hell."[14] Search for the Passage continued in spite of Hearne's "walk," though there was increasing skepticism about the hope of an easy route to the Indies. George Vancouver noted, on leaving Falmouth April 1, 1790,

"No small measure of mirth passed among the seamen in consequence of our having sailed from old England on All Fools Day for the purpose of discovering a Northwest Passage."[15]

They sailed anyway.

The McMillan Trip

In 1824, an HBC factor (chief administrator) from Fort George at Astoria traversed part of the route Puget and Whidbey charted in 1792. James McMillan brought 40 men, including the first American, William Cannon, to dip a toe into south Puget Sound. They pioneered a route north through Shoalwater (Willapa) Bay, along the ocean shore to Grays Harbor, up the Chehalis to the Black River and down from Black Lake to Eld Inlet; they then followed Vancouver's track north to the Fraser River, all in November and December! John Work, who kept the journal, noted the tree-choked condition of the Black River as they portaged their three boats around the impassable stretches. This route became one highway between Astoria and Puget Sound, used for commerce and social visits. Seventeen years later, in July of 1841, officers of the Wilkes Expedition, including Passed Midshipmen Henry Eld and George Colvocoresses, and assistant botanist William Brackenridge, followed part of the same route, from Nisqually to Grays Harbor, by canoe.[16]

Manifest Destiny

The Americans were the ultimate winners of the occupation sweepstakes. The westward flow of settlement, formalized by the concept of "Manifest Destiny," received a boost in the Northwest from an 1818 agreement with Great Britain that allowed joint occupancy of the Oregon country.[17] With hindsight, it is obvious that the logistics of the flow of settlement from that time left only the question of when the territory would become American. The issue seemed in doubt, nonetheless, from the near view as President Martin Van Buren sent Wilkes' six ships on a four-year voyage of science and exploration. An underlying purpose was certainly to expand the American presence in the Northwest. Van Buren was an opponent of slavery; and the possibility of creating new "free" states in the Oregon country could have been a motivating factor in the President's determination to have the Expedition sail, despite public criticism over the delays under Captain Catesby Jones. When the Expedition returned four years later, John Tyler was President. His states-rights, pro-slavery stance gave him no cause to celebrate the sailors' return, but the flow of settlement had by that time begun, slowly, but inexorably, toward the Oregon country.

The United States Exploring Expedition

The nation was young at the time of the "U.S. Ex. Ex.," as the Expedition was known. The nation had been even younger when Congress first resolved to send an expedition in 1828. Thomas ap Catesby Jones took command when the appropriation was finally made in 1836. Congress had been stimulated to explore by John Cleves Symmes'[18] "holes at the Pole" theory of a hollow earth, by other nations' exploration successes, and by the need for accurate charts of the Northwest coast, expressed by naval officers such as Matthew Maury. The progress of the exploration was beset by extraordinary delays. John Quincy Adams, who was President during the authorization of the Expedition, sat in Congress nine years later. The Expedition was yet to begin, and Adams was moved to remark in exasperation that all he wanted to hear of the Expedition was that it had sailed.[19] Jones was replaced by Lieutenant Charles Wilkes, who proved a match for the bold and competent leaders of other nations' enterprises.

Equipped with six "well-found vessels,"[20] the latest fruits of the technology, several scientists of note, a young and energetic officer corps, and, above all, the single-minded determination and perseverance of Charles Wilkes, the squadron sailed for Madeira, the Cape Verdes, and Rio de Janiero. Secretary of War Poinsett, at a loss to find a senior officer willing to replace Commodore Thomas ap Catesby Jones, elevated Wilkes, a highly qualified surveyor, but an untested squadron commander, to take charge. Overcompensation for his junior status may have been one factor in his irascibility and martinet-like behavior. "If Wilkes were God," jokes Murray Morgan in his *Puget's Sound*[21] "many a saint would have fled Heaven." Part of his command presence may be attributed to heredity: his great-uncle, John Wilkes, an English agitator and reformer, was possessed of unparalleled virulence and wit in his publications and exchanges on the floor of Parliament.[22] John Wilkes' great-nephew Charles possessed at least his uncle's quick reactions to perceived attacks.

As the squadron rolled down the South Atlantic toward Cape Horn and Orange Bay, Wilkes prepared for his first excursion into Antarctic waters, taking four vessels south. With more men under his command than Custer commanded at the Little Big Horn, it could only be expected that the force of Wilkes' personality and the sheer numbers of officers would create factions. Wilkes was perhaps more sensitive to this possibility than a more experienced officer might have been. He perceived a "cabal" of officers critical of his command, among those who had originally been under the command of Commodore Jones.[23] These included Thomas Craven and Samuel P. Lee, mentioned earlier, Lieutenant Long, who commanded the *Relief*, and Lieutenant Claiborne.

After eight weeks in the Antarctic, the Expedition left for the coast of Chile. The *Sea Gull*, with the popular midshipmen Reid and Bacon as officers, was never seen again. *Relief* was sent home from Callao via Sydney, and the squadron, reduced to four, charted the Samoan Islands in the fall of 1839.

The second Antarctic exploration came in the winter (the austral summer) of 1840. While in the Antarctic, Wilkes encountered Dumont D'Urville in the *Astrolabe*.[24] A controversy over which man had first identified the Antarctic Continent raged for a century, and this conflict provided the base for one of the charges brought against Wilkes upon his return to the U.S. Discrepancies in the dates recorded in the logs at first seemed to indicate Wilkes' sightings were a day later than D'Urville's, and Wilkes was accused of falsifying his records in order to take the glory of discovery. D'Urville claimed two sightings, each a day earlier than Wilkes and Ringgold in the *Vincennes* and *Porpoise*. Investigations later showed that Wilkes had adjusted for the international dateline in January, while D'Urville had not done so until June, "five months after the visit to the Antarctic."[25] D'Urville's sightings were thus a day later than Wilkes, who is truly the discoverer of Antarctica. Wilkes charted 1,600 miles of the Antarctic Coast over the following two months; that area now bears the name Wilkes Land.

Vincennes Amongst Ice-Bergs

Orange Harbour, Tierra del Fuego

View of the Antartic Continent

Vincennes in Disappointment Bay

Peacock in Contact With Ice-Berg

The Antarctic venture was a high point for Passed Midshipmen Henry Eld and William Reynolds. On January 16, 1840, they saw from *Peacock's* masthead two peaks, which now bear their names. Inexplicably, Lieutenant Thomas Budd, officer of the deck at the time, failed to log their sightings. This added fuel to the Wilkes-D'Urville controversy.

The squadron next sailed to the Fijis, where a Fiji chieftain, Vendovi, was taken hostage in retaliation for the murder of the crew of the merchantman *Charles Doggett*, in 1834. While in the Fijis, Wilkes encountered Captain Edward Belcher and *HMS Sulphur* on a similar expedition. Belcher was known for his "ill temper and callous treatment of...subordinates"[26] and impressed even the irascible Wilkes by his lack of tact and excess of ill-humor. The Fiji survey included a tragedy which deeply wounded Wilkes' own family. His nephew, Midshipman Wilkes Henry, and Lieutenant Joseph Underwood were killed by Malolo Island natives as they bartered for food. Wilkes did not emulate de La Perouse's "turn the other cheek" policy toward such attacks, but instead retaliated with an assault. About sixty Fijians were killed.

The Sandwich (Hawaiian) Islands were the Expedition's home from September through December, 1840, with a return to the Societies and Samoa in early 1841. Observatories were set up throughout these visits, the most prominent and challenging being that on Mauna Loa.

The Expedition divided, with *Vincennes* and *Porpoise* proceeding to the Columbia River and Puget Sound in April, and the *Flying Fish* and *Peacock* arriving in July of the same year.

The Results

The cruise of Darwin and Fitzroy in the *Beagle* to some extent inspired the sponsors of Wilkes' epic voyage. In some ways, the results of the Wilkes journey were as far-reaching: dozens of young officers trained and motivated—eight admirals, seven Confederate Navy officers, an acting Secretary of the Navy (William Reynolds); scientific careers and theories advanced— James Dwight Dana's plate tectonics, Charles Pickering's ethnographic studies, Horatio Hale's linguistics, Joseph Drayton's engravings; the Smithsonian Institution launched, enhanced by the sheer volume of journals and collected specimens overflowing the capacity of the Expedition's temporary repository in the Patent Office; the establishment of the National Botanic Gardens; and the unmeasurable but undeniable effect of the Northwest explorations on the negotiations with Great Britain on claims to the Northwest. President Tyler, though concerned over the non-slavery/ slavery balance, thought enough of Wilkes' report to send it to Congress with this message:

"In pursuance of the suggestions contained in the accompanying letter from the Secretary of the Navy [Abel P. Upshur] and of my own convictions of their propriety, I transmit to the Senate the report made by Lieutenant Wilkes, commander of the exploring expedition, relative to the Oregon Territory. Having due regard to the negotiations now pending between this Government and the Government of Great Britain through it special envoy, I have thought it proper to communicate the report confidentially to the Senate."[27]

And again, what of Wilkes, this mix of irascibility and competence, determination

Vendovi

Vendovi

and precipitous behavior? His crew members described him often in terms like Lieutenant Reynolds, "a rascally tyrant, liar, black-hearted enough to be the Devil's brother"[28] and as often having the determination and buoyancy of a cork. He was all of these, and arguably, in the face of the scope and challenge before him, the right man for the job. The face and future of our Pacific Northwest was shaped by his energy and dedication.

The Ships

What were the tools available to these voyagers? The fundamental tool was the hull; the vessels that bore the voyagers over a four-year span. The original flotilla, under command of Captain (courtesy rank, Commodore) Catesby Jones was:

> *Macedonian* (frigate), Commander James Armstrong
>
> *Relief* (storeship), Lieutenant Thomas A. Dormin
>
> *Consort* (brig), Lieutenant James Glynn
>
> *Pioneer* (brig), Lieutenant William D. Newman
>
> *Active* (schooner), Lieutenant William Woolsey[29]

The *Macedonian* was considered to have too great a draft for inshore work, and the brigs and the schooner were worn out. Only the *Relief* was retained, earning on the voyage the designation of "slowest sailor." The *Active* (schooner) preceded the steamer of the same name on the Navy list. (The steamer *Active* was later commanded by Lieutenant James Alden of the Expedition on his return to Puget Sound in 1855.)

The replacements for the first consignment included the following:[30]

Vincennes, launched 1826, sloop of war, 127-foot length, 700 tons. Served through the Civil War and sold in 1867. Known as a "good sailer." Sailed on the first U.S. Arctic Expedition, Cadwalader Ringgold, 1853. Cruised the Pacific, 1834, Captain J. H. Aulick (later commander advising the Wilkes Expedition. Officers included Passed Midshipman Matthew F. Maury.

Peacock, launched 1828, sloop of war, 600 (or 650) tons, 118-foot length. Among the first of the "rebuilt" ships a new ship designed by Humphreys, she was built retaining the name of the old sloop *Peacock*, because funds were provided by Congress for repair but not for construction.[31] This evaded the legal question of proper authorization. This system reached "extraordinary" proportions in the post-Civil War periods of corruption within the government. Twenty-two guns, often rated at 18. Lost on the bar of the Columbia River, 1841.

Porpoise, brig, launched in 1836, 88-foot length, 224 tons. Rigged originally as a brigantine, rated twelve guns, reduced for surveying. Commanded by Wilkes in 1837 survey of Georges Bank, 1851 John Taylor Wood (later captain, Confederate States Navy, served aboard during anti-slave running patrol). Lost in the China Sea, 1854.

Observation and Recording of Mirage near False Cape Horn and Hermit Islands

Relief at Noir Island

Sea Gull and *Flying Fish*, schooners, 110 tons and 96 tons. Former New York pilot schooners, 70-foot length, crew of 15. *Sea Gull* lost off False Cape Horn, 1839, *Flying Fish* sold in Singapore, 1842.

Relief, ship. Storeship, sent home from the Expedition with "dissidents" in 1839 from Callao. One hundred nine-foot length, 470 tons. Very slow sailer.

Oregon, brig, 250 tons, 85-foot length. Merchant ship bought in the Columbia to replace the *Peacock*, remained on the Navy List after the Expedition.

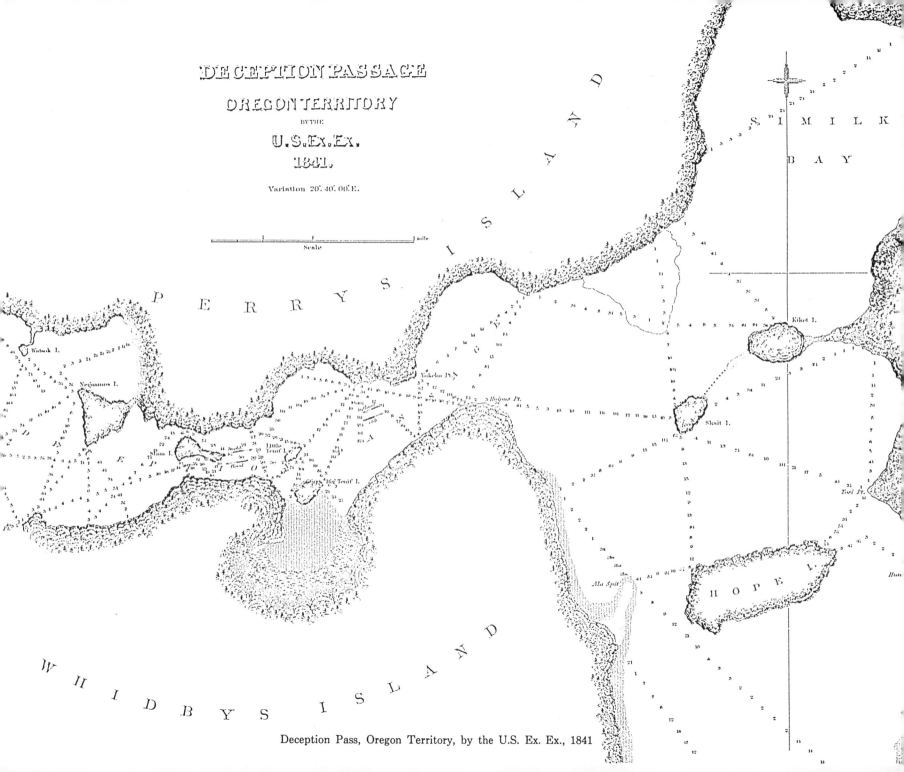

Deception Pass, Oregon Territory, by the U.S. Ex. Ex., 1841

Science and Technology

Navigational instruments and ships' equipment available to the sailors of the mid-19th century were advanced far beyond those available to the early explorers of the Northwest coast. The 18th century invention and development of the jib sail, the chronometer, signal flag codes, and the theodolite,[32] (a device which measures azimuth and horizontal bearing on the same instrument—Wilkes would have his theodolite eyepiece stolen by Indians during his Puget Sound surveys) gave Wilkes the ability to navigate, chart, and communicate with great accuracy and clarity. Wilkes used a very rapid triangulation method involving use of the measure of the speed of sound for one arm of his survey triangles (the offshore arm). By shooting off a gun at one end of the line, then timing the interval between the "flash" and the "bang" at the other end, Wilkes' surveying parties could swiftly and accurately measure distances over water. Wilkes' charts were so accurate that they remained in use for a century. The World War II landing on Tarawa (in the Gilbert Islands in the south Pacific) was carried out with the aid of a Wilkes chart.

With the "base-by-sound" method, Wilkes' surveyors could complete a running survey of a seven-mile-long island in three-and-a-half hours. The Expedition's thematic charts became definitive references in several fields, such as Wilkes' "Map of the World Shewing [sic] the Extent and Direction of the Wind and the Route to be Followed in Circumnavigation of the Globe."

Technological and scientific advances enabled Wilkes to employ rather complex astronomical observatories throughout his voyage, in such locations as Mauna Loa in Hawaii and at Nisqually. Another notable and unusual (for his time) scientific practice was Wilkes' venture to "Bute Prairies" (Mima Mounds) in what is now southwest Thurston County, on May 20, 1841. He opened three of these "tumuli" which he described as "conical mounds thirty feet in diameter and 6 to 7 in height, but nothing was found in them."[33]

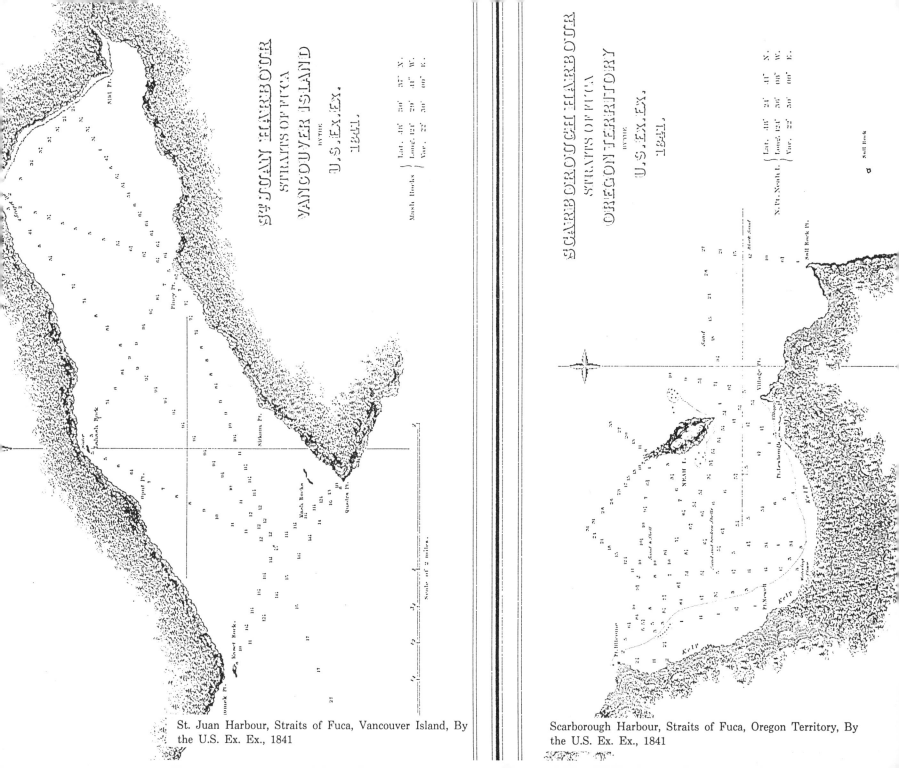

St. Juan Harbour, Straits of Fuca, Vancouver Island, By the U.S. Ex. Ex., 1841

Scarborough Harbour, Straits of Fuca, Oregon Territory, By the U.S. Ex. Ex., 1841

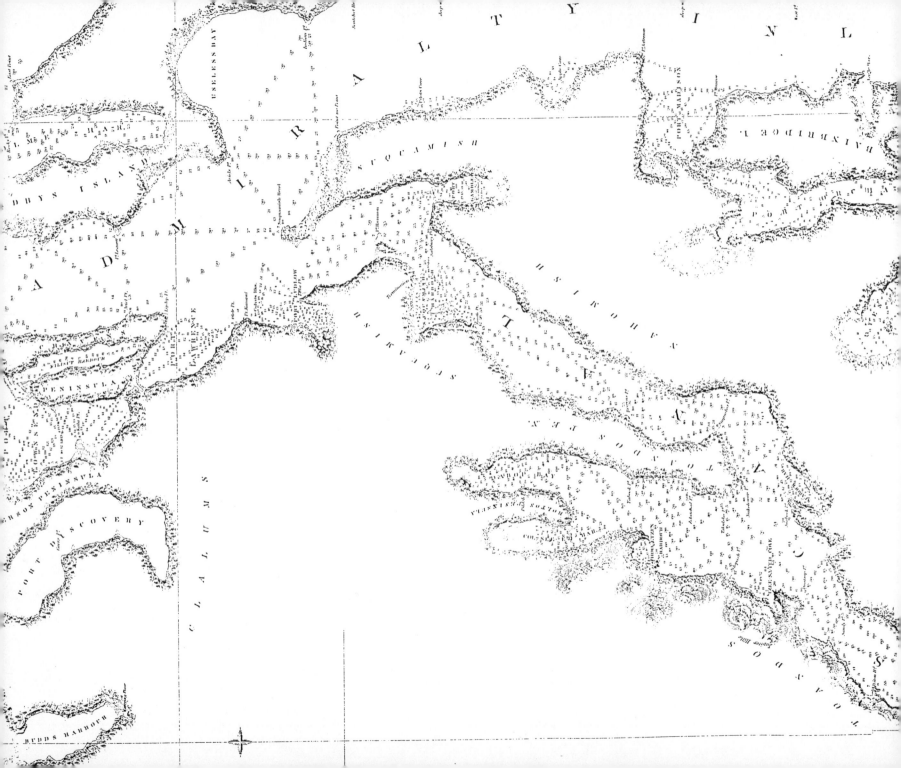

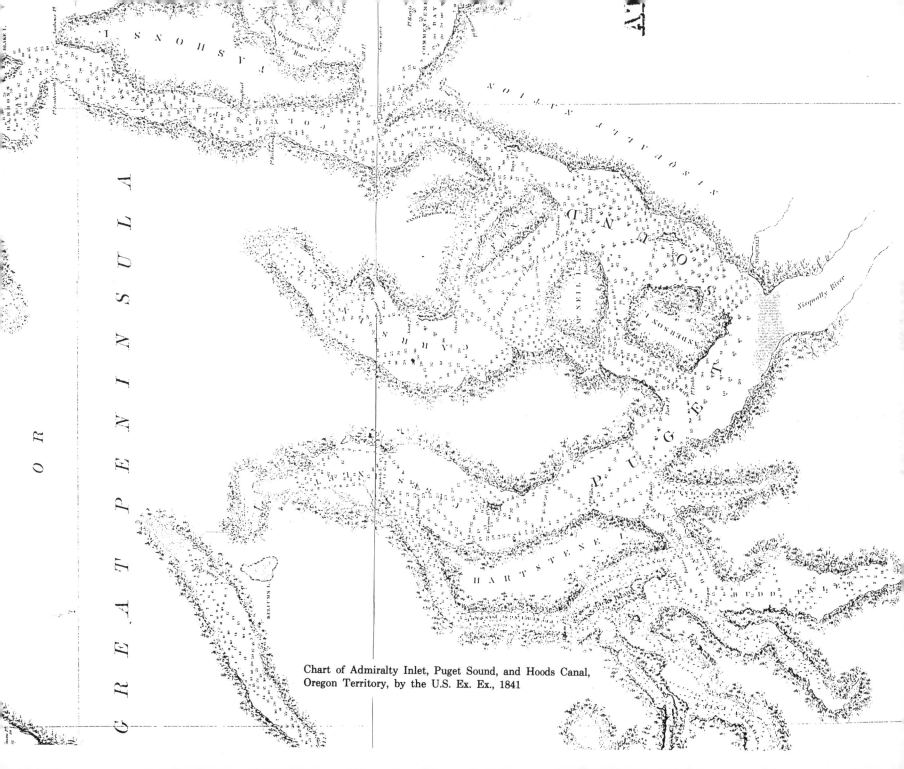

Chart of Admiralty Inlet, Puget Sound, and Hoods Canal,
Oregon Territory, by the U.S. Ex. Ex., 1841

"THOUGH FAR FROM OUR HOMES, YET STILL IN OUR LAND"[35]

by

Frances B. Barkan

By the time the United States **Exploring Expedition arrived in the Puget Sound region, the general** outline of the landforms was known, and there were numerous American and British settlements in what is now Oregon and Washington. The missionaries, settlers, and Hudson's Bay Company employees had added to the fund of knowledge about the geography of the Oregon country, and there was little trail-breaking to be done. The Exploring Expedition would not be seeking the local equivalent of the source of the Nile, or the location of the South Pole. Instead, the Exploring Expedition's contribution to the body of knowledge about the Northwest was more subtle, more detailed, providing the ingredients to stir the Oregon country into the American pot, tying into the whole of the nation its obscure Pacific corner.

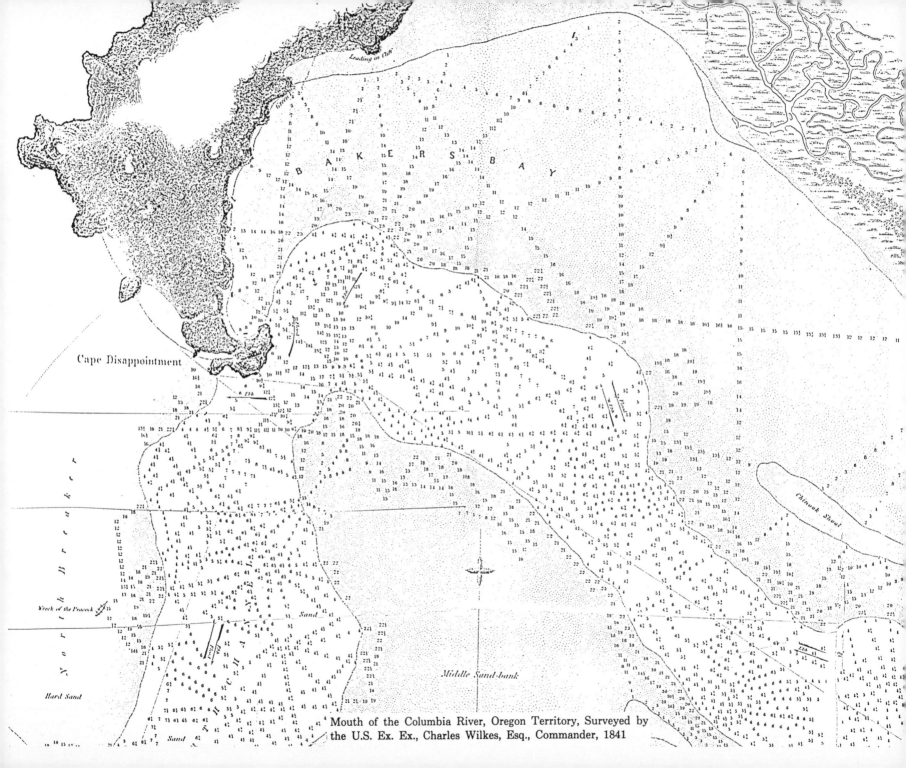

Leading in Cliff

B A K E R S   B A Y

Cape Disappointment

Chinook Shoal

Wreck of the Peacock

North Breaker

Hard Sand

Sand

Middle Sand-bank

Mouth of the Columbia River, Oregon Territory, Surveyed by
the U.S. Ex. Ex., Charles Wilkes, Esq., Commander, 1841

First Approaches

Charles Wilkes, United States Exploring Expedition commander, planned a survey of the Columbia River, which meant attempting a crossing of the fearsome sandbar across the river mouth. When he arrived on the Oregon coast, near Cape Disappointment, on April 28, 1841, he wrote

"I, notwithstanding, stood for the bar of the Columbia river, after making every preparation to cross it; but on approaching nearer, I found breakers extending from Cape Disappointment to Point Adams, in one unbroken line."[1]

He noted that Captain George Vancouver, who had preceded him in the exploration of the inland waters of Washington, had doubted the existence of the Columbia.

"I am at a loss to conceive how any doubts should ever have existed, that here was the mouth of the mighty river, whose existence was reported so long before the actual place of its discharge was known, or how the inquiring mind and talent of Vancouver could have allowed him to hesitate, when he must have seen the evidence of a powerful flood of fresh water contending with the tides of the ocean, in a bar turbulent with breakers, in turbid waters extending several miles beyond the line of the shore, and in the marked line of separation between the sea and river water."[2]

Vancouver's doubts about the existence of the river were not shared by other explorers, and the traders and settlers who followed them, and there were now settlements both at the river mouth and upstream. Wilkes wrote about the conditions of the bar, urging great respect for the unpredictability and violence of the water.

"Mere description can give little idea of the terrors of the bar of the Columbia: all who have seen it have spoken of the wildness of the scene, and the incessant roar of the waters, representing it as one of the most fearful sites that can possibly meet the eye of the sailor. The difficulty of the channel, the distance of the leading sailing marks, their uncertainty to one acquainted with them, the want of knowledge of the strength and direction of the currents, with the necessity of approaching close to unseen dangers, the transition from clear to turbid water, all cause doubt and mistrust."[3]

Wilkes decided not to wait for the bar to clear, and instead laid his course north for the Strait of Juan de Fuca. He would complete the survey of the river later. The weather was murky, but with little wind, and the two ships almost came to disaster when they sailed close to the rocky, steep shore. However, they were able to round Cape Flattery and make the entrance to the Strait.

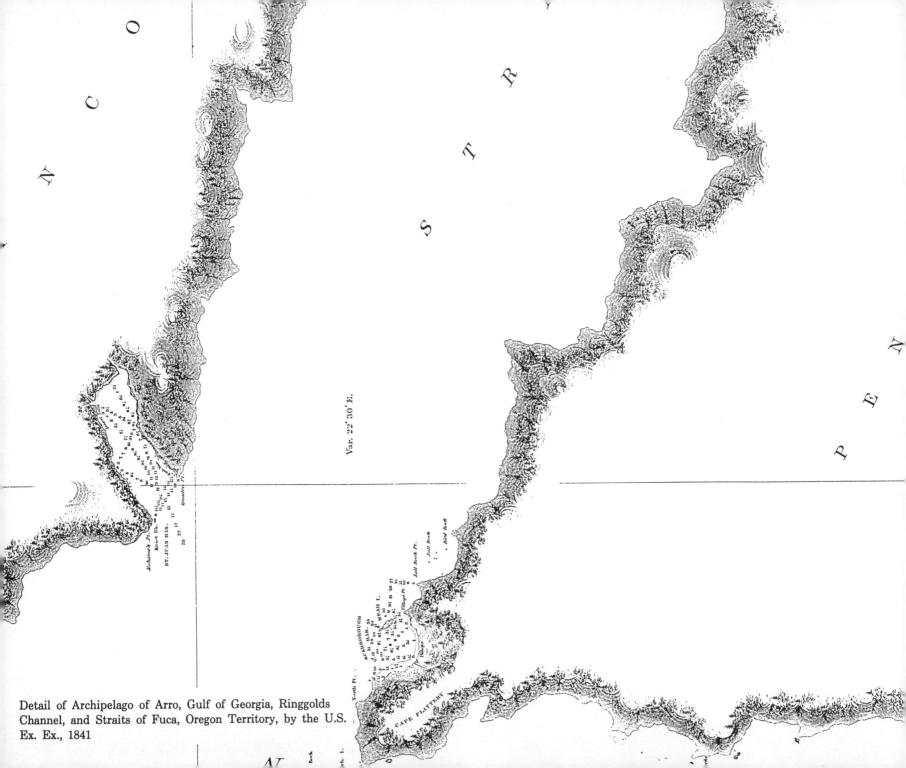

Detail of Archipelago of Arro, Gulf of Georgia, Ringgolds
Channel, and Straits of Fuca, Oregon Territory, by the U.S.
Ex. Ex., 1841

In his diary, Wilkes repeated a strange story he heard while in the Oregon Country.

"It was also near this spot, that the very remarkable occurrence of the wreck of a Japanese junk happened in the year 1833. The officers of the Hudson's Bay Company became aware of this disaster in a singular manner. They received a drawing on a piece of China-paper [rice paper], in which were depicted three shipwrecked persons, with the junk on the rocks, and the Indians engaged in plundering. This was sufficient to induce them to make inquiries; and Captain M'Neil was despatched to Cape Flattery to obtain further information, and afford relief, should it be needed.

"He had the satisfaction to find the three Japanese, whom he rescued from slavery; and the Hudson Bay Company with characteristic liberality, sent them to England."[4]

Light winds kept the ships from reaching Cape Flattery until the last day in April. Wilkes reported that they were forced to tack up the Strait, as they could find no appropriate anchorage near the mouth, and that this difficult passage was made at night. However, the entrance to the Strait is free from shoals and other dangers, and by daylight the ships were well within the safety of the inland waters.

Pipes of the Northwest Indians

Indian Mat Hut

Indian Burial Place, Oregon

Tatooche Chief

Wilkes had access to the charts and journals of his predecessors, and was especially grateful for the pioneering work Captain George Vancouver had done in 1792. On May 2, Wilkes' ships anchored in Port Discovery (now called Discovery Bay), named by Vancouver in 1792, and Wilkes wrote

"...we hastened to reach Port Discovery, where we anchored at half-past 6 p.m. on the 2nd of May; just forty-nine years after Vancouver, pursuing the track of De Fuca, had visited the same harbor."[5]

Wilkes relied on Vancouver's charts to get him from the northern part of the Sound to Fort Nisqually; these charts provided a portrait of the waters he intended to explore, and Wilkes used names Vancouver gave to bays, points, and other features. That he appreciated Vancouver's thoroughness and attention to detail is obvious from his comments, such as this one about Port Discovery:

"The description of Vancouver is so exactly applicable to the present state of this port, that it was difficult to believe that almost half a century had elapsed since it was written."[6]

and

"It would be difficult to imagine a more perfect harbor than this there appears to be one objection to it the water is rather deep. there never was an island that better deserved its name than Protection Island."[7]

Wilkes used Vancouver's nomenclature on his charts and in his Diary, and added to it names of his own devising, especially in the southern reaches of the inland waters. Wilkes also adopted names given by both white and native local residents or by earlier land explorers. (In some cases, his charts and maps may have been the first "official" recognition of names in use by local residents.)

De Fuca's Pillar

Canoe of Oregon Indians

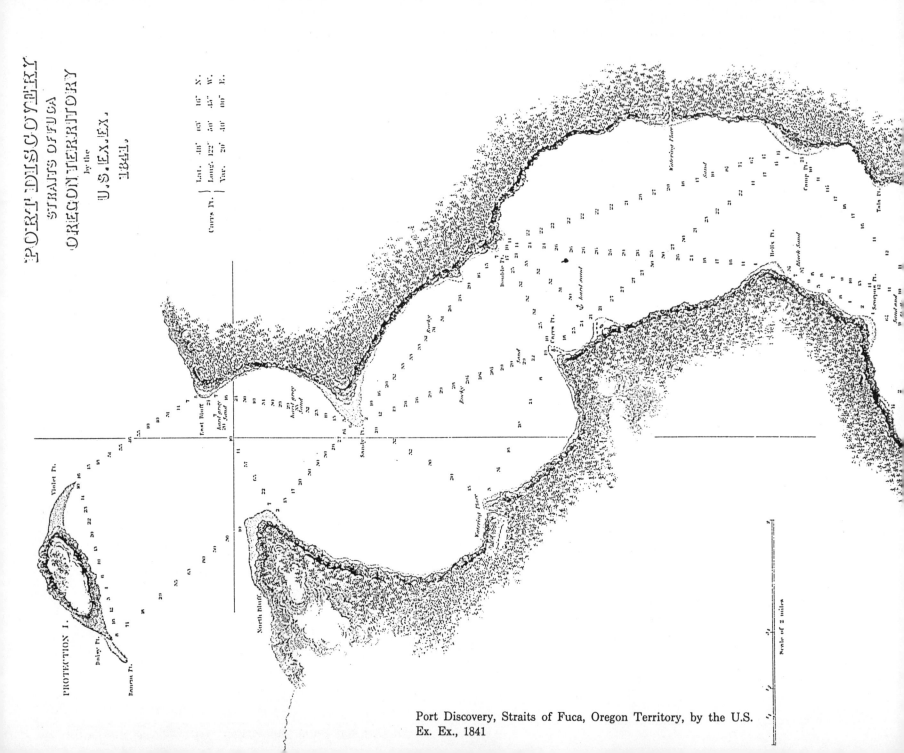

Port Discovery, Straits of Fuca, Oregon Territory, by the U.S.
Ex. Ex., 1841

The Meeting At Fort Nisqually

The Americans were visited by Indians of the Clallam tribe, and Wilkes spent some time observing and recording their artifacts and their customs.

"The two sexes of all who visited us were dressed almost alike, and can hardly be distinguished in external appearance from each other: both wear their hair long, and both are equally dirty...They live principally on fish, shell-fish, the cammass-root, and potatoes...Besides the ornaments we saw among our first visitors, some wampum-belts and strings of dentalium-shells were observed. They have a great passion for carved pipes, for which they cultivate small quantities of a species of tobacco...The women are seen to be weaving mats, after the Chinese fashion, of bullrushes (Scirpus lacustris), which they place side by side and fasten together at intervals...The canoes of this region differ from anything we have seen on the voyage. They are made from a single trunk, and have a shape that may be considered elegant, and which is preserved from change by stretching or warping by means of thwarts..."[8]

Wilkes sent an Indian to request a pilot from the Hudson's Bay Company post at Nisqually, just south of the Tacoma Narrows. After a few days, he decided his message had gone astray. An energetic surveyor, Wilkes did not let his crew idle away the wait. He sent charting parties throughout the anchorage, spending the time in confirming Vancouver's observations and adding some of his own.

"All the navies of the world might be furnished with spars here...Fish we have in abundance Salmon, Cod, flounders, Clams, crabs, oysters (small), ducks, geese, Venison..."[9]

He set sail for the South Sound on May 5, and described Port Townsend as

"...a beautiful Bay and had a long level beach with a Pond of Freshwater backing it and a run into the Bay where vessels may be supplied the Point a low sandy one called Hudson's point [in honor of his compatriot on the Expedition, Lieutenant William Hudson] is bold to and may be passed about a 1/4 mile in 10 fathoms from our anchorage Mount Baker shows over Hudson Point a large fleet might anchor and maneuver here, there is a Bluff that joins the beach abreast the ships the top of which slopes to the water and is a beautiful lawn here and there with groups of trees and to the N^d and W^d a fine copse of pine trees upwards of 1000 acres all ready for the plough the soil is a light sandy loam but seems exceedingly productive the grass was several inches high & covered with flowers & wild strawberry plants in blossom."[10]

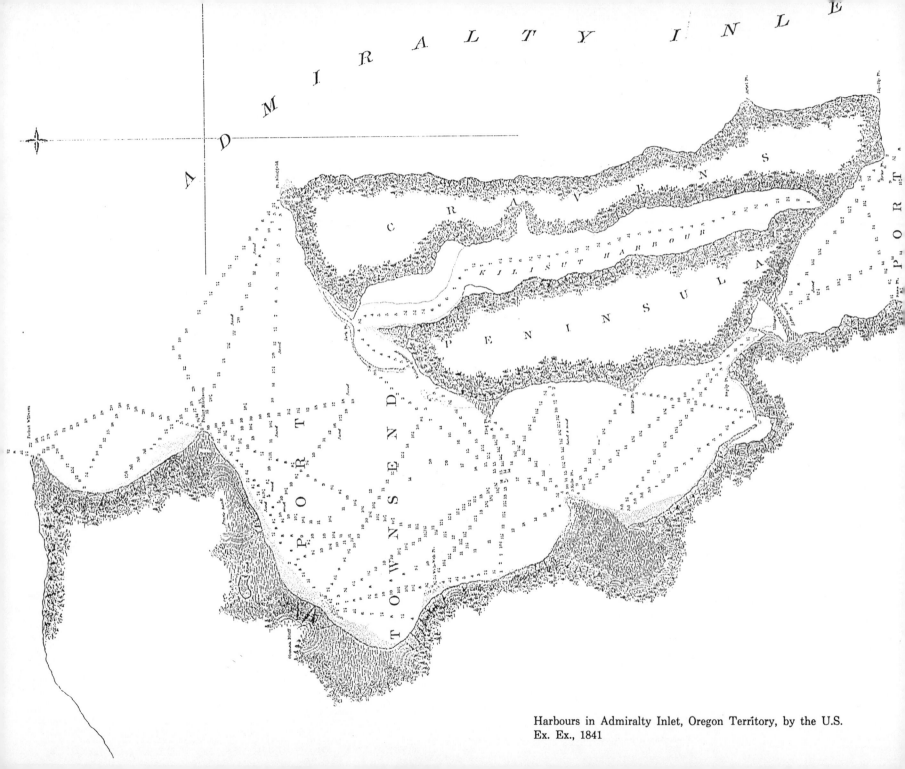

Harbours in Admiralty Inlet, Oregon Territory, by the U.S.
Ex. Ex., 1841

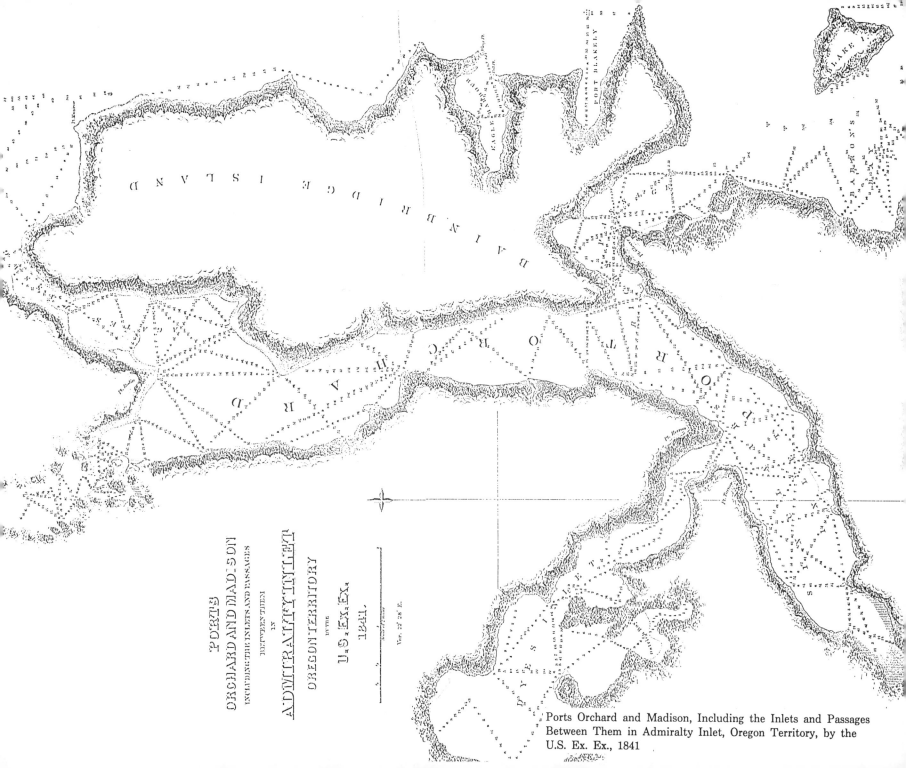

Ports Orchard and Madison, Including the Inlets and Passages
Between Them in Admiralty Inlet, Oregon Territory, by the
U.S. Ex. Ex., 1841

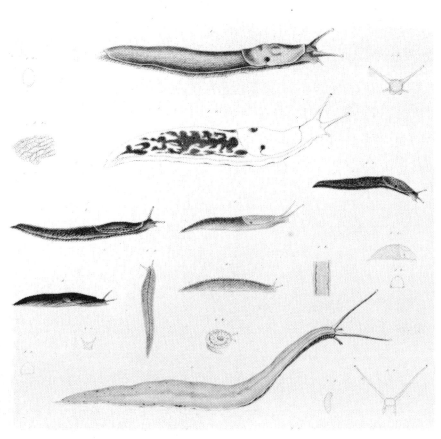

Plate I, Atlas to Volume XII,
Mollusca And Shells
Washington State Library

As the ships went south, they made stops to survey and make charts. The scientists aboard occupied themselves with the collection of specimens. On the 8th, while the ships were on the west side of Whidbey Island, north of the present site of Seattle, the Expedition was joined by the pilot, a Mr. Heath, first officer of the Hudson's Bay Company steamer *Beaver*, moored at Fort Nisqually. Before attempting the passage through the Tacoma Narrows, the Expedition anchored for the night on the west shore, most likely near the entrance to Gig Harbor. Wilkes was determined to survey this part of the Sound, as

"...I deem it highly important as vessels are likely to be detained here in consequence of the difficulty of getting through the Narrows..."[11]

The Narrows notwithstanding, Wilkes liked what he saw of the inland waters, as he commented,

"Nothing can be more striking than the beauty of these waters without a shoal or rock or any danger whatever for the whole length of this Internal Navigation the finest in the world accustomed as we are to prize that of our own country."[12]

On the 11th, the ships arrived at Fort Nisqually, where they were cordially greeted by Captain McNeil and Mr. Anderson of the Hudson's Bay Company; it can be presumed that each side did its best to impress the other.

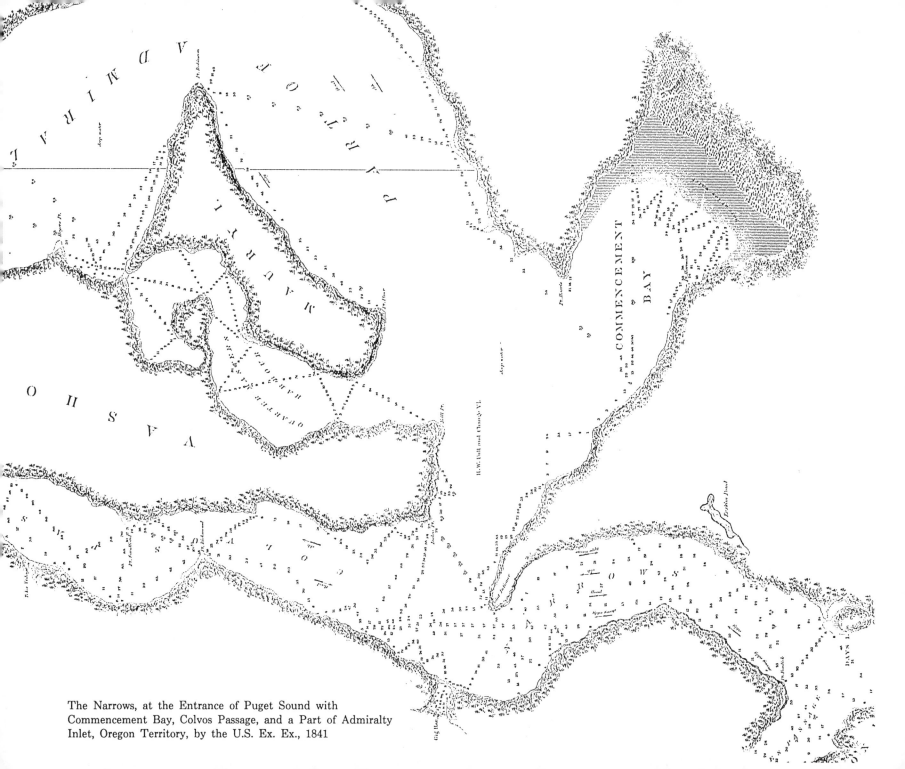

The Narrows, at the Entrance of Puget Sound with
Commencement Bay, Colvos Passage, and a Part of Admiralty
Inlet, Oregon Territory, by the U.S. Ex. Ex., 1841

The Work At Nisqually

Once the Expedition's ships were settled at Nisqually, Wilkes immediately set to work, beginning an ambitious program of surveying on both sides of the Cascade Mountains, throughout Puget Sound, down the Cowlitz to the Columbia and then to the river mouth, and overland to the coastal bays.

"Having arranged my plans, I proceeded forthwith to put so much of them as lay within my own means into execution: the *Porpoise* and boats were prepared for surveying, and the land parties organized...The *Porpoise*, with two of the *Vincennes'* boats, under Lieutenant-Commander Ringgold, were directed to take up the survey of Admiralty Inlet. The launch, first cutter, and two boats of the *Vincennes* were placed under the command on Lieutenant Case, to survey Hood's Canal. The land party intended to explore the interior, was placed under the command of Lieutenant Johnson of the *Porpoise*, Mr. Brackenridge, Sergeant Stearns, and two men. Eighty days were allowed for the operations of this party, which it was intended should cross the Cascade range of mountains, towards the Columbia, proceed thence to Fort Colville, thence south to Lapwai, the mission station on the Kooskooskee river, thence to Wallawalla, and returning by the way of the Yakima river, repass the mountains to Nisqually.

"The other land party consisted of Messrs. Drayton and Waldron of the *Vincennes*, myself, and two servants. Our intended route lay across the country to the Columbia river. First, I proposed to visit Astoria, then Fort Vancouver, and the Willamette settlement, and to proceed up the river as far as Wallawalla. From Astoria I proposed to send parties from the *Peacock* into the interior, and to set on foot the survey of the Columbia river, by means of her boats.

"The establishment of an observatory also claimed my attention: a suitable site[13] was found on the top of the hills, within hail of the ship. Here the instruments and clocks were landed, and put up in a small clearing, when the trees had been cut in order to supply the steamer with fuel.

"All these preparations occupied us until the 15th, when the brig was reported as ready, and sailed the same day."[14]

Wilkes spent some time observing the fort at Nisqually, and described it in detail. In addition, he was much taken with the richness of the farmland and the surrounding countryside, and wrote extensively about its beauty and abundance.

"It [the fort] is constructed with Pickets some 20 feet high quadrangular with Bastions at each corner covering less than an acre sufficient however to accommodate the first Establishment but this having become one of their (H.B.Co.) farms they find it very much contracted...

"...Our route lay through the most beautiful park scenery with the prairies here and there breaking through the magnificent pines...

"our route lay through the gigantic fine cedar forest and although they are called sapplings, were 6 1/2 feet in diameter and upwards of 200 feet in height. I could not control my astonishment.

Pine Forest, Oregon (drawn by J. Drayton)

Foothills, Mt. Rainier (Joseph Drayton sketch, 1841. Oregon Historical Society, negative number orhi 46188)

"...took our departure exclaiming at the beauty of the Park scenery. It was almost impossible to realize our being in a savage & wild country & it but wanted some building country seats to assure us that art not nature had perfected the landscape here.

"The mildness of the day & the freshness of everything around us from the last night's shower added additional beauties to the glowing scenery. Our route lay through alternate prairies & magnificent forest of tall pines and cedar passing by fords several fine streams of water. The soil excellent the prairies were covered with strawberries inviting one to dismount occasionally...There are many plants that excite a feeling of interest in this country as well as known friends at home among the number...

"...I reached the Company's [Hudson's Bay Company] farm on the Cowlitz occupying an extensive prairie, and covered with luxuriant crops of wheat, and affording a pleasing prospect to the eye with its extensive granaries & shed and the litter of straw showing the product of last year's crop and the industry of civilisation in the distance on some of the free settlers with their log huts & young orchards attached putting us in mind of our Western States with the exception however of the remains of the conquered forest, here the ground is ready for the plough and nature seems as it were to invite the husbandman to his labor."[15]

Wilkes received a warm welcome and considerable assistance from the Hudson's Bay Company employees stationed at Nisqually. For his own part, he found their company stimulating and pleasant; in addition, he recognized that his voyage through the Oregon country would be much more difficult without their help.

"Left the fort at Nisqually at 10 A.M. [May 19 for Astoria]. Our party consisted of Mr. Waldron Mr. Drayton myself and three servants with a guide (Canadian) and two Indian boys and together with our baggage horses they amounted to 13 all of them kindly loaned to me by the Company's agent Mr. Anderson in charge of the fort to whom I feel under many obligations for the trouble he took in fitting us out, if it had not been for his kindness we should have made sorry work of it..."[16]

Though he was impressed with their horsemanship, Wilkes saw little else to praise about the Native Americans he encountered. Like many of his time, Wilkes had negligible understanding of and empathy with the native cultures of the places he visited. These attitudes were common among educated Americans and Europeans, who held the ethnocentric view that their own culture represented a higher state of development than those of non-whites. This prejudice extended not only to material artifacts and achievements, but also to the realm of thought, the arts, religion, and language.[17]

Wilkes found it not particularly regrettable that some tribes had vanished or were on the verge of disappearing, due to disease, war, and other causes.

"The Indians belong to the Klackatat tribe, though they have obtained the general name of the Cowlitz Indians. In a few years they will have passed away, and even now, I was informed, there are but three Indian women remaining in the tribe."[18]

Early in his stay at Nisqually, he expressed admiration for the way Indians rode their horses, though he also noted that, by his standards, they were cruel to their beasts.

"the management of their horses is truly surprising, and those that a foreigner would be unable to get off a walk they will mount and proceed with speed without the aid of spur or anything but a small switch...The horses appear to me to have a knowledge of an indian and his cruelties to them. The usual bridle is simply a piece of rope fastened to the under jaw which seems all sufficient for the management of the most refractory horses and so different from the Spanish bit that was ever looked upon as necessary in such cases that one is not a little surprised how they are enabled to overcome them. They practice great cruelty in using their animals & a horse is seldom found that has not a raw back.

"The Indians of this country are so much with their horses that one ought in giving their character to separate the two. On his horse he is a man but dismount him, and all his qualities vanish & he becomes the lazy, lounging lout insensible to anything but his own low gambling habits.

"In traveling in this country when it becomes necessary to use horses one must lay aside all his feelings relative to means of his conveyance whether on sore backs, jaded horses, or those that are lamed and half starved, these will accompany him wherever he goes my advice to all is to keep away from your horses until they are saddled."[19]

Indian Horses Near Mt. Hood (Joseph Drayton sketch, 1841,
Oregon Historical Society, negative number orhi 46189)

This cultural blindness had a terrible effect on both conquered and conqueror. It resulted in the decimation and destruction of native cultures and peoples by Europeans and Americans, because it was assumed that these societies had no value. What is more, those who held the view that native cultures had no significance were diminished by their inhumanity and indifference. Ironically, they missed the opportunity to learn from native inhabitants much of practical importance.[20]

Indian Mode of Rocking Cradle

To The Mouth of the Columbia

The trip to Astoria and the Columbia River was easy, traveling a well-used route from the southern end of Puget Sound. Wilkes and his companions camped out some nights, but were sometimes able to take comfort at Company farms and missionaries' houses. Most of the Company farms were, in fact, tiny settlements, with extensive agricultural operations and small surrounding communities of a few houses. Wilkes was able to supply his expedition with necessities and acquire guides. Though his route lay through unoccupied territory, it cannot be said that this was a wilderness excursion.

For part of the way, the expedition's route followed the Cowlitz River, which flows into the Columbia. Wilkes and his men took to canoes, for the journey down the Columbia to Astoria, leaving their horses at the Company's farm on the Cowlitz. Along the way, Wilkes observed the country, and made an observation on the weather in the region.

"The weather is not actually cold nor is the winter long, snow seldom lays but a day or two, fires are necessary most months in the year—"[21]

Female Costume

Male Costume

Wilkes was curious about virtually everything, and made notes in his diary about local Indians, the yields from Company farms, procedures used to tan deer hide, geology, plant life, and a multitude of other facts about the country.

"I will give here the mode of preparing buckskin which may be termed the cloth of this country. 1st. Immediately after the deer is killed the skin is taken off & stretched tightly over a frame after having all the hair scraped off, it is left until it becomes as dry as parchment, it is then rubbed over with the brains of the animal which imparts the oil to it then it is steeped in warm water, after which it is dried over a fire two women stretching it all the time it is drying and smoking, it is then again wet and stretched by winding tightly round a tree, from which it is again drawn & dried over the fire by women pulling it as before, when dry or nearly so, it is rubbed with the hands as in washing, until it is soft and pliable and is then ready for use.[22]

Wilkes' curiosity and his predilection for detail led him to look into the navigability of the rivers, and resources the country offered settlers, such as coal, timber, and farmland.

"When the river [the Cowlitz] is high it can be navigated by boats drawing 5 or 6 feet of water, the entrance from the river (Col[a]) [the Columbia] is barred and would admit of but a small draft of water for sea going vessel it may be said to be unnavigable 9 months of the year & small steamers might be enabled to do it a month or two longer.

"The route by the Cowlitz will always be the general one by which the communication with the Northern Section of the country will be kept up at any rate until the country becomes settled—by it all the mountain ranges are avoided & the highways provided by nature (the river) point out the best course—to avoid and pass them."[23]

and

"...unlike our great River of the Eastern side it [the Columbia] bears no fertilizing earth for the planters, but acts by its flood, upon his exertion to prevent his crops from coming to maturity...[the annual flood] is enough to destroy the coming crop the icy water chilling and preventing the grain from ripening...

"...no copper is found south of 59 degrees N. in this territory where the pure copper is found in abundance and which the natives beat into large sheets which are articles of trade on the coast & are there sometimes met with traders.

"Coal is said to be found near the foot of the Rocky Mountains, on the Cowlitz and at Vancouver Island specimens of the two latter I have seen and obtained that of the Cowlitz Lignite but from Vancouver Island it is a good quality bituminous coal."[24]

As Wilkes' little band traveled down the Columbia, they met with the brig *Wave*, which had brought Expedition supplies from Oahu to Astoria. She was to carry a cargo of lumber back to the Hawaiian Islands, marking the early days of what has become a continuing trade for Washington and Oregon—shipping lumber or logs to Far Eastern ports. He reported that the lumber commanded $80 per thousand board feet, and that about 20 men were employed in cutting the timber. Wilkes spoke to the master of the *Wave*, and was disappointed to learn that the *Peacock*, which he had been expecting daily, had not yet arrived in Astoria. The fate of the *Peacock* was to cause Wilkes considerable worry during the next few weeks, and, unfortunately, his worst fears were to be realized—the *Peacock* was lost on the Columbia bar.

Astoria was disappointing to Wilkes, in that

"...the few buildings (log houses) appear to be going rapidly to decay the Company appearing to pay little regard to them, they do not appear to have done anything since the establishment was moved to Victoria, the opportunity of farming being very limited and the clearing expensive now has endeavored to be established and perhaps as it is avowedly on the American side of the River it is thought unnecessary to continue operations that could not be permanent."[25]

Astoria had been founded by American fur traders, directed by John Jacob Astor. However, during the 1812 British-American war, the American residents sold the fort to the British Northwest Company (a rival of the Hudson's Bay Company later united with the HBC), fearing a bloody takeover by British ships and troops. Though the fort was handed back to the Americans in the Treaty of Ghent (1815), it was primarily a British settlement, as few American citizens remained in the area. By the time Wilkes arrived, even the British were slowing down their operations in the area, finding their farms at Vancouver and on the Cowlitz more productive and a better investment.

Wilkes traveled around the area, as he wanted to determine the size of the bay at Astoria, and he also wanted to see Fort Clatsop. In addition, Wilkes wanted to look into coastal defenses for the Astoria area. The party spent a few days in the area before Wilkes started for Vancouver. He left behind Waldron, who was to wait for the *Peacock*; in addition, he had an opportunity to send a letter to Washington, D. C., reporting on his progress to date. Though he was only 3,000 miles from the nation's capital, the letter had to take the long way around, reaching Washington via the Sandwich Islands.

Concomely's Tomb, Astoria (drawn by A. T. Agate)

Fort Astoria

Vancouver

The trip to Vancouver was taken in easy stages, and in a few days, Wilkes and Drayton arrived at the HBC's farm. Wilkes was greatly impressed with the size of the operation, and with Dr. McLoughlin, who was in charge of the facility for the Company.

"He is a fine looking person of robust frame, with a frank open countenance about 50 years of florid complexion his hair white is a Canadian by birth of Scotch parentage enthusiastic in disposition and I should think of great energy of character and well suited for the situation he occupies which requires no small talent and industry to fulfill."[26]

Wilkes went on to describe in detail the farm. Officially, the farm was owned and managed by the Puget Sound Agricultural Company, an organization whose principal stockholders were Hudson's Bay Company officials. Hides and tallow were sent to England, and the farm traded with the Russian American Fur Company, which represented Russian interests in Alaska. Wilkes was told that the farm contained about 3,000 acres, and he commented that in his opinion,

"...this country is better adapted to the raising of cattle than even California and not so subject to drought, the cattle in consequence of the climate are better able to bear the weather, are larger and stronger."[27]

Wilkes also noted that the Company was hosting several missionary families which had arrived in the Oregon country by wagon train across the Rockies. These families had little employment, and, according to Wilkes, lived on the charity of the Company. Wilkes requested information from them about the country—soil conditions, weather, and other physical data—but remarked that he

Fort Vancouver

Willamette Falls

Fish-Hooks

Indian Dice

"...found them possessed of little information respecting the country having kept no notes or made any observations relative to the soil temperature climate what observations they did make unsatisfactory explanations about the country and certainly not to be relied on, therefore I have put little or no confidence in what I gathered from them..."[28]

The daily routine of the farm was another item Wilkes described in his diary.

"At early dawn the bell is rung for the working parties and soon after all are at work. The sound of the hammer clink of the anvil and rumbling of cart wheels was a great novelty to us and not an unpleasant one after so long an absence of it and so unlike the notes of the morning in the forest—at 8. the bell is again rung & all go to breakfast at nine they are again at work which continues until one an hour for dinner all dine and again at 6 when the labours of the day close. This is the amount of employment and every one is busy indeed. Vancouver is no place for an idle person destitute of amusements except reading."[29]

Wilkes remarked on the situation of the employees of the Company, noting that

"The servants of the Company are engaged for 5 years and after that time has expired the Company are under bonds to return them to England or to the Canadas in case of cruises. They received as I said about 17 pounds each & are fed when their time expires almost all are in debt consequently they are obliged to serve an extra time on the expiration of which they all as formerly have long since married an Indian or have had children & find themselves unable to leave & whilst they so continue they are as it were still bound to the Company and still under their *surveillance*."[30]

Wilkes stayed at the Company's farm for several days, scrutinizing every aspect of the operation and making detailed notes in his diary. He was obviously impressed with the size and the yields of the HBC's farms. In addition, he made notes on the Indian salmon fishery, local plant and animal life, the fur trade, the Indian population of the Oregon country, and the missionaries (including Marcus Whitman, perhaps the most famous missionary of the era).

"The salmon fishing is now in its most active operations at the Cascades & Willamette falls and this draws the Indian population far and near to it. the tribe in whose territory or limits they are exact a tribute to all who fish, the general average price of a salmon is 10 cents tho' this will depend very much upon the wants of the Indians. They refuse to sell any Salmon until after the first run and then always without the heart they have many superstitions in relation to them some of which I will give from the best authority I could derive them, but I am nevertheless well satisfied that there are very few who can understand these languages sufficiently to obtain them & I further believe that very few of the Indians now living are aware of or have any knowledge of their traditional stories.

"Rode...to see the Fort Dairy...they now have about 300 brood mares, about 2500 sheep 3000 cattle, there were 70 milch cows at the dairy...

"The Company in order to avoid losses by the desertion of their men generally send them in large parties from 30 to 40. When they take their wives & families with them and trap during the season on some favorable ground where they remain for the season, they leave in October & return again by May or June. They usually trap on shares & this is according to the skill of the trappers.

"The country remarkably healthy grass in Feby—& the pasturage for cattle good requires no housing they feed upon the tufts of grass that by the heat of the sun are converted if I may so express it into natural hay.

"The saw mill is two miles farther and likewise on the banks of the Col[a] [Columbia River] ...it has several runs of saws and is as fine a pile as I have seen anywhere, and in few countries could such material be procured for the framing of any building...The description of the timber used for cutting into boards is far inferior to what we should deem merchantable in the United States being of the quality or little better than our hemlock.

"A small manual labor school is kept here for the education of the orphans and 1/2 breeds of the Company's servants and will be of much service to the rising flock. There are at present 23 boys. An examination of them was had altho they did not prove very expert at their exercises in reading & writing yet it gave sufficient evidence of their improvement to show that they were in a fair way to acquire the rudiments & some allowance was to be made as they had been for some weeks constantly employed in the field under their teachers."[31]

Wilkes made estimates of Indian tribal populations, and determined that about 20,000 Indians lived in the Oregon country. He included in his count Nez Perce Indians from Idaho, as well as certain Plains tribes that made periodic excursions to the eastern part of what is now Washington. In addition, Wilkes notes that there were about 350 whites living in the country, including Hudson's Bay Company servants and officers.

Indians Playing the Spear Game, Foothills of Mt. Hood (Joseph Drayton sketch, 1841, Oregon Historical Society, negative number orhi 46190)

To The Willamette

After several days, Wilkes set out to see the Willamette settlement, a collection of small farms and missions located up the Willamette River from the present site of Portland. (These communities, near Willamette Falls, eventually incorporated in towns such as Oregon City and Champoeg.) The American settlers here were eager to meet with Wilkes to get his opinion on their desire to form a government. Wilkes, for his part, was interested in making a full report to his superiors, which would of necessity include detailed information on all settlements and communities in the Oregon country.

Wilkes traveled to the Oregon settlement by flat-bottomed boat, ordinarily used for transporting grain or other commodities. These boats were ideal for the relatively shallow Willamette. On the way, Wilkes ran into a group of eight Americans who were building a schooner to take them to California. The builders had been in Oregon for about a year, but had decided to move to California, as they were disappointed in the Oregon country. The eight eventually sailed to California, where the schooner was sold; the party purchased cattle and drove them back to Oregon. Wilkes wrote that he was "proud of the spirit they evinced" in their building project, saying that they carried on their plan "so truly in character with their countrymen."

Wilkes found, when he landed at the settlement, that he was to be placed in an awkward predicament. The local residents were eager to form a provisional government, and they wanted Wilkes' opinion about the validity of their idea. His point of view was greatly valued, as Wilkes represented, in the settlers' minds, the government in Washington, D.C. However, Wilkes was extremely skeptical about the necessity of any government, and advised the residents to drop the idea. An extensive entry in his diary lays out his reasons.

"A committee waited on us of 5. principally the lay brothers of the Mission to consult and ask my advice relative to the establishment of the laws after hearing attentively all the arguments that were produced in favour of it, and which as I think might be summed up in a few words having no substantial reasons for it, crimes do not appear to have been committed as yet & the persons and property of the settlers is fully secure it appeared to me that their reasons were principally that it would give them more importance in the eyes of others and induce in their opinion settlers to flock thereby raising the value of their farms and stock. Seeing this view of the subject I disagreed with them entirely in the necessity and policy of adopting any

1st. Because of their want of right, and those wishing for laws were in fact a minority of the settlers.

2nd. By their own accounts they were not necessary yet.

3rd. They would be a bad substitution for their moral code, which they now all follow, and that few who were disposed to do wrong would be willing to settle near a community of whom a large portion was opposed to evil doing.

4th. The great difficulty there would be in enforcing the laws, and defining the limits over which they should extend. would the Hudson B. Company be willing to enter into their enactment? Respect the Laws? No.

5th. Not being the act of the Majority, & the larger part of the population being Catholics they must at once produce discord, & be of great detriment or injury to the settlement.

6th. Besides I thought it would produce an unfavorable impression at home hearing the missionaries were alone in making the request for laws thereby admitting that in a community avowedly brought together & under their control they had not enough moral force to prevent crime, & therefore must have recourse to a criminal code. From my observation I was well satisfied they were unnecessary and could not avoid drawing attention to the fact that after all the various offices were filled there would be no subjects for the law to deal with. These arguments had the desired effect, for I understand they have been entirely dropped since."[32]

Wilkes noted in his Journal that he "advised them [the settlers] to wait until the government of the United States should throw its mantle over them."[33] Many on the Expedition shared this conviction that the Pacific Northwest belonged to the United States. Wilkes said in his Journal that

"There were many things to remind us of home: among them was a luxuriant sward of white clover, now in full blossom, and numerous other plants that had found their way here: the trees were also familiar, and truly American. I felt that the land belonged to my country, that we were not strangers on the soil; and could not but take great interest in relation to its destiny, in the prospect of its one day becoming the abode of our relatives and friends."[34]

A piece of doggerel written by R. P. Robinson, Purser's Clerk on the *Vincennes* no doubt expressed the feelings of many of the crew.

"Though far from our homes, yet still in our land

True Yankee enterprise will ever expand,

And publish to all each side of the main,

We triumphed once and can do it again.

A problem, a problem, oh! hear great and small,

The true owners of the country are still on the soil,

While Johnathan and John Bull are growling together

For land which by right belongs not to either.

Let philosophers listen, and solve the question

Which has troubled the statesmen of each nation,

By what right the "Big Bull" claims sustenance here,

While he has plenty of pasturage elsewhere."[35]

Older men in the Expedition's crew could have served in the American Navy during the War of 1812, only thirty years before, and some had fathers or grandfathers who had fought against the British in the American Revolution. The Hudson's Bay Company's activities in the Pacific Northwest may have given the impression that the British were interested in repeating the colonial experiment started two hundred years ago at Jamestown. There was a palpable British presence on the continent in the Canadian colonies, which lent weight to the idea that America might have to assert her sovereignty once more.

In his diary and Journal, Wilkes praised the efficiency of the Company's operations and the HBC employees he met at Nisqually and further south. Interestingly enough, he found most Americans he encountered—almost all missionaries—less than acceptable. These missionaries he said, were doing little to

Old Mission-House, Oregon

accomplish their appointed tasks. Wilkes apparently did not question the need for missionaries, nor, for that matter, did he assume that missionaries as a class were less than respectable; in fact, he had expressed great admiration for several he had met in the South Seas. However, he did contrast the HBC employees and what he considered lesser American efforts. In addition, his comments, particularly in his Diary, give the impression he thought many of the Americans incompetent at best.

"I could derive little or no satisfactory information relative to their views and prospects in forwarding the education of the Indians from what tribe they proposed taking them and the matter of teaching &c. &c. from all that I did hear however my impression is that there is not field for the numbers that are now attached to this mission & in a very few years none of this army will be left. They seem not to wish to push their Missionary operations to the North where the tribes are numerous and extensive & the climate is healthy...I view it a great neglect on the part of this mission if they have not made true representations at home respecting their prospects & it seems to me unaccountable how they can have received so large an amount of funds without having done more than is apparent or acknowledged by themselves...Something may be said that these missionaries came out under the idea that they are to settle and afford the necessary instruction if possible, but they are to colonize under the christian religion as their law and guide & give the necessary instruction to the tribes they settle among to train them up in good habits &c. &c. how this is to be done without exertions strenuous efforts I am at a loss to conceive and it strikes me as obligatory on these Missionaries to state the facts they one and all admit."[36]

Later, Wilkes said of another missionary settlement that

"These missionaries are very far from what they ought to be low, vulgar and unclean. I am invited to partake of their hospitality including all those about us. I have seldom if ever until I came here witnessed so much uncleanliness, & so little regard paid to proper decorum if they were Christian men and readers of their bible, they ought to practice cleanly habits. Mr. W. [a missionary] was as filthy as any Indian I have met with in appearance & taking our nation into consideration more so They are sent out to show an example but how little they do in this respect and how they earn their wages in preaching the Gospel a higher and Just God will determine from this I must exempt the wives who I must say are in a great degree the honor of their husbands & my only wonder is that they dont insist upon the adoption of their habits by them."[37]

He went on to comment about the differences between Canadian and American settlers in the Willamette Valley.

"I find in the Willamette a great difference in the two classes of settlers Those composing the Canadian Population and the American cheerfulness and industry are well marked in the appearances of the former while neglect & discontent, with lou[n]ging seem to infect the latter."[38]

As was his practice, Wilkes made observations about the countryside, the weather, and the crops produced by local farms.

Plate 3, Atlas to Volume VIII, *Mammalogy and Ornithology* (Special Collections Division, University of Washington Libraries, negative number UW 2734)

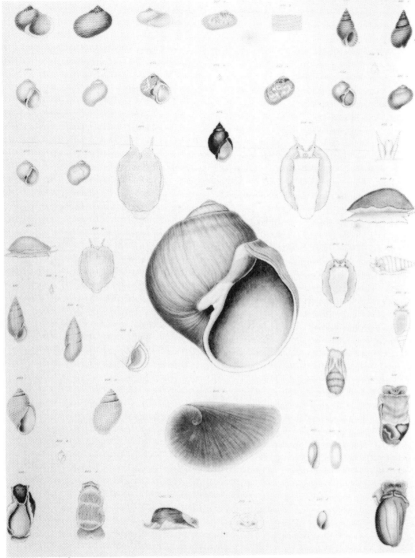

Plate 15, Atlas to Volume XII, *Mollusca and Shells*
(Washington State Library)

"One of the most striking appearances of the Willamette Valley is the flatness of its prairies in some instances a dead level for miles in extent—and it becomes a problem of some difficulty to solve how they have been produced. Fire is no doubt the cause of their being kept clear of an under growth and may have been the original cause of them but the way the forests are growing around them would almost preclude this supposition as but thin belt of wood frequently occurs between extensive ones.

"The rains are mild seldom any hard showers the winter of 1840 was thought to be the most severe of any yet known by the oldest white inhabitant. They had a foot of snow it laid but a few days, the coldest time of the year is said to be the end of Jany. or by beg^g Feby. The thermometer has been known to fall as low as -8 degrees zero but for a very short time the N.E. and Easterly winds are the most unpleasant coming from the mountains, but a short dist. they produce sudden and great changes in the temperature. The S ^{d} & SW^d winds are the warm winds although they generally bring rain or mist. Those from the N ^{d} & W ^{d} fine clear weathers. Westerly winds are the most prevalent."[39]

Wilkes and Drayton stayed at the Willamette settlement for a few days, collecting data and making observations. Wilkes even attempted to obtain the partial skeleton of a mastodon; unfortunately, the bones, which had been unearthed at one time, had been reburied. Wilkes regretfully abandoned the effort to add the bones to the ships' already-bulging store of specimens.

Wilkes traveled to Willamette Falls, and from there descended the Willamette to its mouth at the Columbia. Drayton was left behind temporarily to collect more specimens and to make drawings of various objects.

Fort Vancouver Again

At Fort Vancouver, Wilkes met Peter Skene Ogden, a Hudson's Bay Company factor who had been in the Oregon country for over thirty years. Wilkes said that

"I have been exceedingly amused since my return to the fort with the voyageurs of Mr. Ogdens party. They are to be seen lounging about in groups decked off with feathers ribbons &c. &c. with the conceit and flaunting air of a finely dressed country girl evidently looking down upon all those employees who with their somber and business like air are moving around the fort as if they were total strangers to the pleasure of life while these jovial fellows seem to have naught to do but att. to the d[eco]rating of their persons and pleasures" [40]

Wilkes spent some time talking with Ogden about Company operations and profits, and commented that

"I cannot but view the Industry and labours of this Company as but tending to forward greatly the advantages to be derived from it by the future possession of the soil—enabling emigration to go on with much great ease profit and rapidity. From the nature of the country its peculiar adaptation to grazing, mildness of its climate, and the little attention required for the care of Herds I am satisfied that this must become one of the richest cattle companies in the world and go far to compete with any portion of it, in its salted beef, Pork, & for which the climate is deemed exceedingly favorable."[41]

In his diary, Wilkes made other notes about agricultural crops, some of which have become important to the modern economy of the region.

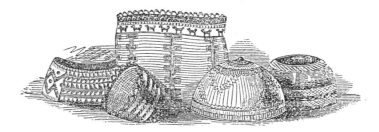

Indian Baskets of Oregon

"...the climate is well adapted for fruits particularly apples pears & grapes have been tried but do not yet yield well figs are grown also, and some very fine melons rasberries currents & strawberries are also fine...Potatoes are planted in the fields & enormous crops are had...One of the gentlemen...introduced Hops by bringing a few living plants with him from Canada..."[42]

Wilkes also noted that

"The resources of these Rivers cannot be well estimated in their salmon and would afford a large source of profit to its Settlers."[43]

Wilkes was constantly thinking about his two missing ships, worrying whether they had made it to the Columbia. He wrote orders for their commanders, and had left Waldron in Astoria to await their arrival. By this time, the ships were long overdue, and Wilkes feared they were lost at sea. Wilkes also arranged for Drayton, who had rejoined him, to accompany Peter Ogden to Walla Walla; Ogden's boats would carry Wilkes as far as the Cowlitz settlement.

Wilkes regretted leaving the congenial company at Vancouver, but was touched by the ceremonial parting.

"about 10 o'clock we were all summoned by Dr. McLoughlin to the Hall to take a parting cup customary in this country and observed as far as I could learn throughout among themselves...Some no doubt think this piece of Scotch politeness would be better in the Breach than observance but I was of a very different opinion it whiles away that part of leaving of ones friends that is always the most painful the pledging of each other, and the good wishes one takes with him are all pleasant and give a warmth to recollections of by gone days that is by no means

disagreeable, one feels and loves the kindness, and attention to ones friends to the last, & enables one to bid goodbye with more courage—I like this hanging to old customs with the Scotch, perhaps more attended to than any other nation, and there is always a warmth of feeling thrown into its observance that cannot but be felt."[44]

The voyage to the Cowlitz was swift, and Wilkes was impressed with the voyageurs' skills.

"The management of the Boat in the rapids (though on a small scale) of the men truly surprised me and how well trained & dexterous the canadians are in using the Pole & paddle and withal so jovial singing almost the whole time one or the other of them, & then all joining in chorus giving them spirits & serves to keep them awake, & make the time pass quickly."[45]

Return to Nisqually

After a day at the Cowlitz farm, Wilkes started the return journey to Nisqually on June 23. He was pleased to find, on his arrival, that much of the work he had assigned was completed, and that news of the surveying parties was good.

For several days, Wilkes occupied himself with experiments and projects. An oven was built to bake bread for ships' stores, Wilkes made observations of various stars, calculating the latitude, and he directed other officers in charting and surveying. The altitude of Mt. Rainier was measured, and Wilkes mentioned in his diary that he concluded the peak was 14,850 feet tall, less than 500 feet in error. These activities occupied the officers and men until July 4.

Mount Rainier

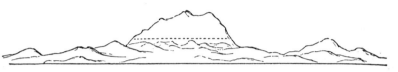

Mount Rainier

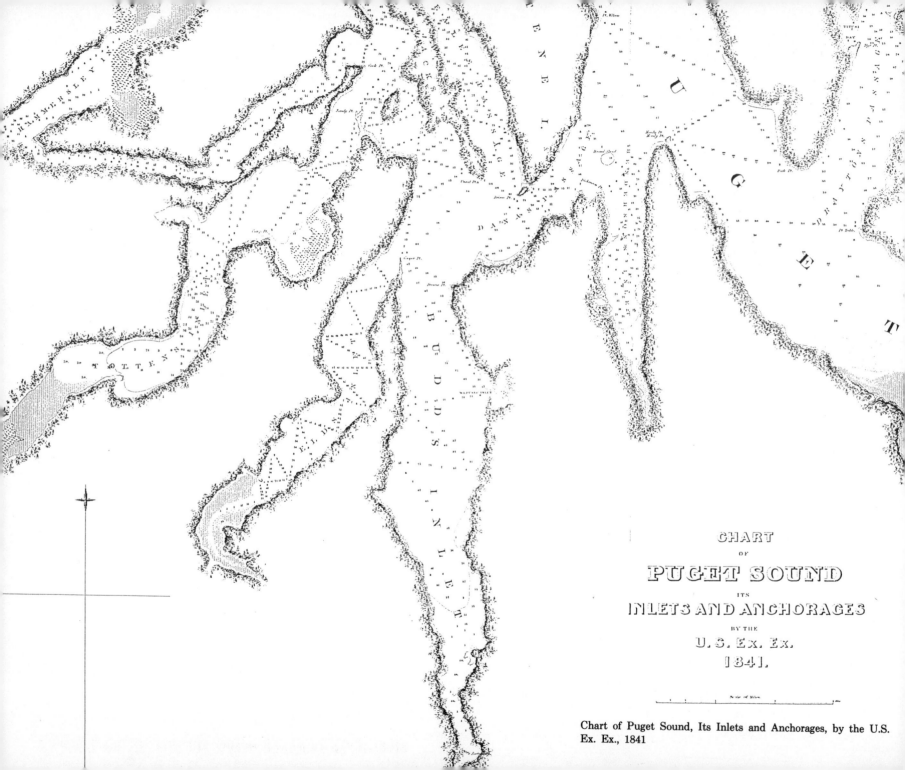

Chart of Puget Sound, Its Inlets and Anchorages, by the U.S. Ex. Ex., 1841

The Fourth of July Celebration

Wilkes intended to celebrate the 4th in a suitably impressive manner, and ordered all the surveying boats to return by that date. As the 4th fell on a Sunday, the actual celebration was held on the 5th, though the officers and crew spent the 4th making ready.

Wilkes described the day:

"Crew were mustered on board & came on shore in their nice clean white frocks & trousers with the marines in uniform & music & after forming at the Observatory they marched off under M^r. B. [Passed Midshipman Thomas A. Budd] & Colv. [Passed Midshipman George W. Colvocoresses] to the Prairie where the preparations had been making. It was truly a gratifying sight to see them all in good health not a man sick and as white as the driven snow with happy & contented faces. on their arrival partners were chosen and the games began including horse racing &c. &c. At noon on firing the 2nd. salute with the Brass Howitzer a Q. G. [quarter gunner] by the name of Whitehorn had his arm dreadfully lacerated by the accidental discharge of the gun. The D^r. thought amputation necessary but to this I objected as it could as safely be performed in a few days as now and might [not] be neccssary. he was sent off in a Barrow to the ship with his ship mates. This accident put a momentary stop to the Hilarity but as Jack [the sailors] is somewhat familiar to such scenes it was soon forgotten and they resumed enjoying their sports until near sunset when they again formed & returned on board with their music all in good order...These frolics and exercise tend to do the crew good and after so long a cruize I feel it great recreation to my own mind to see all those enjoying themselves who have passed with me through so many dangers, and by their exertions achieved for the Country no small reputation."[46]

Wilkes was so pleased with the results of the Expedition to date that he unbent enough to start the football game the men and officers played in the meadow. The officers were invited to dine with their commander, and Wilkes included in his invitation the Hudson's Bay Company officials who had been so hospitable to the Expedition.

Chinook Lodge (drawn by A. T. Agate)

The Eastern Washington and Grays Harbor Expeditions

While Wilkes was occupied in Nisqually and along the Columbia, other officers and crew members were surveying in Eastern Washington and traveling to the Pacific Coast. The results of these two expeditions added greatly to Wilkes' reports about the Oregon country and its conditions.

The Eastern Washington group left on May 19, crossing the Cascade Mountains and heading northeast to Fort Colville and Fort Okanogan. The itinerary called for them to travel south to the Walla Walla area, then return to Nisqually via a more southerly pass in the Cascades. Wilkes had given orders to make extensive observations on a variety of subjects, including the specifics of the terrain, natural objects, daily temperatures, height and circumference of unusual trees, and bearings on the North Star and the sun.

Needless to say, the ships' officers who headed the Eastern Washington voyage were more accustomed to managing sails than managing horses on slippery mountain trails. Nonetheless, they crossed the mountains in good order, augmenting their supplies with food purchased from Indian tribes they encountered on the way. The men stopped at Forts Okanogan and Colville, Hudson's Bay Company posts, and were assisted in their travels by the Company's employees. Their route crossed some of the most spectacular country in the state, including the area around Grand Coulee. After visiting the Lapwai Mission and Walla Walla, they returned to Nisqually July 15.

Fishing-Huts at The Dalles

Fort Wallawalla

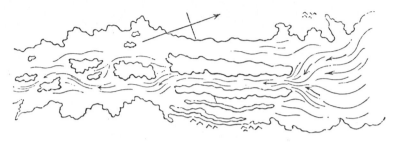

Columbia River Rapids

Skin Lodge

Drayton had been sent to Walla Walla with Peter Skene Ogden, and he arrived just after the departure of his colleagues. Wilkes wrote extensively about this trip in his Journal, contrasting conditions at Nisqually with those in the drier and hotter eastern part of the state. Drayton returned to Nisqually at the end of July, after visiting several mission stations (including that of the famous missionary, Dr. Marcus Whitman). With Drayton's data, Wilkes was able to complete a map of the entire course of the Columbia in Washington.

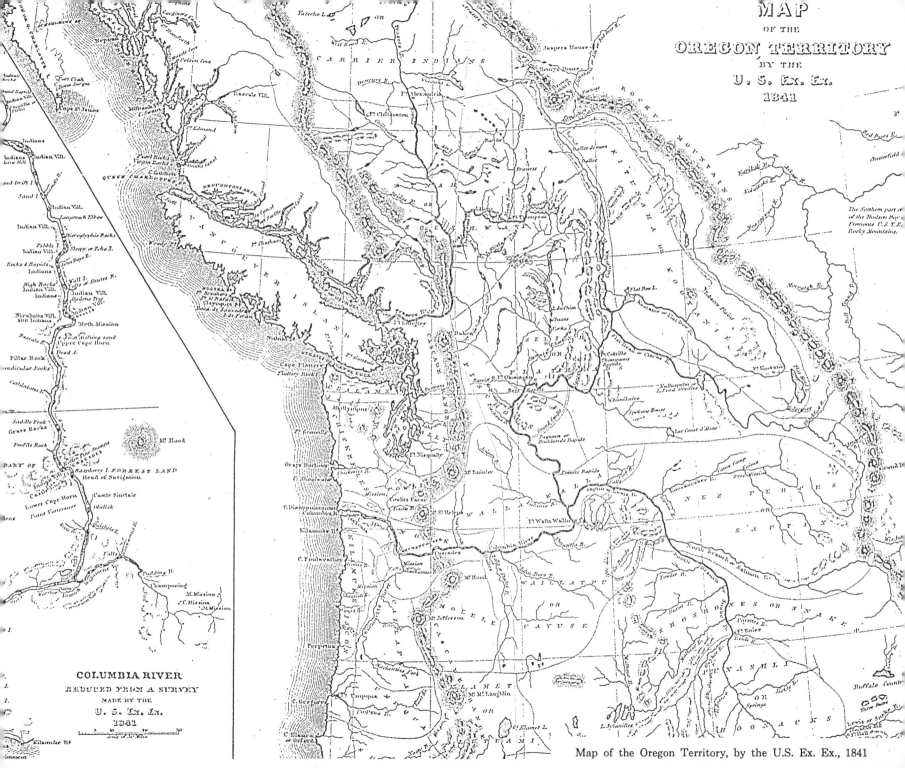

Map of the Oregon Territory, by the U.S. Ex. Ex., 1841

Salmon Fishery in Chickeeles [Chehalis] River

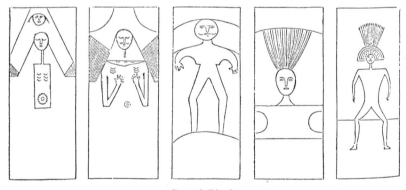

Carved Planks

The Grays Harbor expedition was carried out after the 4th of July celebration and the return of the Eastern Washington crew. Wilkes gave orders for the expedition's members to travel to the coast, survey the harbor, and then rejoin the ships at Astoria; he then sailed for the Strait of Juan de Fuca. The trip to Grays Harbor was through difficult country—not mountainous, but thickly wooded. The group canoed down the Chehalis River and some of its tributaries to reach the harbor, which is the outlet of the Chehalis.

The survey of the harbor itself was hard, and the harbor proved to be too shallow for commercial ship traffic. The members of the expedition had problems obtaining canoes from the local Indians, and ran low on supplies. When Wilkes arrived in Astoria, and realized the Grays Harbor crew had not yet made the rendezvous, he sent out a search party with supplies. The men rejoined their colleagues at the end of August.

With these two surveys in hand, Wilkes was able to present a fairly complete portrait of Washington—including physical characteristics and already-existing settlement patterns. His information on routes, flora and fauna, and terrain were invaluable to new settlers, as well as to those seeking "the mantle of the United States."

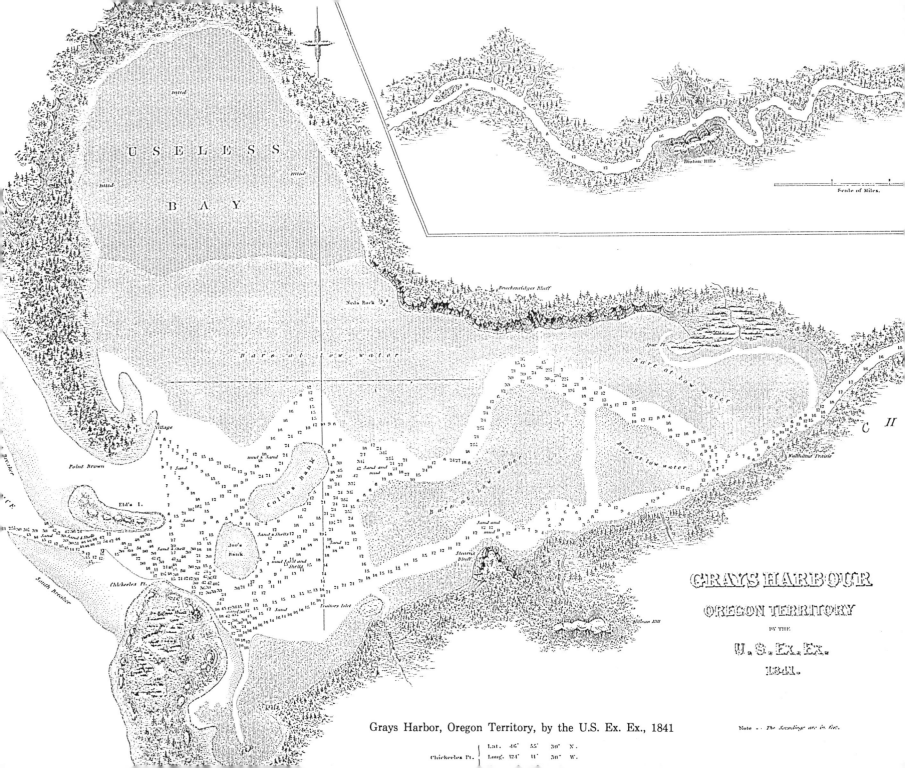

Grays Harbor, Oregon Territory, by the U.S. Ex. Ex., 1841

Note -- *The Soundings are in feet.*

Last Days At Nisqually

After the 4th, Wilkes felt it was time to conclude his observations and leave. He dispatched officers and boats on surveys of the southern inlets of the Sound, and decided to attempt to solve the mystery of the mounds on Butte Prairie (now known as Mima Mounds). Wilkes had passed these strange objects on his way south a few weeks earlier, and was determined to find whether they were natural, or were instead burial mounds of early Indian tribes.

"...chose the Butes that we desired to open 3 of which were dug into. They are composed of alluvial soil apparently by the soil being brought together, and are remarkably rich of a mellow black mould. Their dimensions are generally 15 feet in diameter and six feet above the gravelly soil—about one might be placed every four thus [a drawing was inserted here]...the whole prairie is covered with them almost all perfect in their form, the subsoil a hard reddish gravel...No kinds of articles, bones or anything was found in them—This was the case in many parts of the country, the Indians having no tradition respecting them whatever. On the many inquiries made I could get no surmises even respecting them. In their absence will attempt a suggestion myself. They are not tumuli [burial mounds] not are they held in any regard by the Indians. I did learn however that the Medicine men were in the habit of gathering some herbs from them, and it may be the continuance of a practice that has been handed down to them to do...They seem fit places for the growth of various herbs & might have been the custom for each tribe or family to cut its own...They lie in a flat prairie and are thousand in number with great regularity in their rows

Bute Prairie

liking them to familiar object to everyone I would say they are prodigious *corn hills* with quite their regularity and from the great numbers of them must have been a herculean labor—"[47]

For the next several days, Wilkes and his officers surveyed the southern inlets and made ready their departure. Wilkes made some final observations of the terrain, the Indian tribes, and the tides.

"These arms of Puget Sound bear very much the same character The soil is light on a subsoil of sand & gravel The banks in some places about 100 feet covered with spruce, pines, oaks, alders & arbutus great quantities of seringas in full blossom reminded us of home, and although not partial to its smell heretofore it was found by all of us delicious it savoured of civilization...

"Tide rises 18 feet spring tides and about 12 ordinary or neap tides H. water full & change 6.10 p.m. During all the time of our stay at Nisqually there was found to be a great discrepancy between the night and days tide the former not being so high by 2 feet. This was also the case in the Columbia...

"The Indians around Nisqually are few in numbers & a lazy vicious set and exceedingly dirty. They for the most part sleep all day & sit up all night gambling with visitors or among them and in this way like all tribes of this coast they will after parting with all their useful articles dispose of their wife & children & finally of themselves to years of Slavery...They are addicted to stealing and will run some risk to effect their object..."[48]

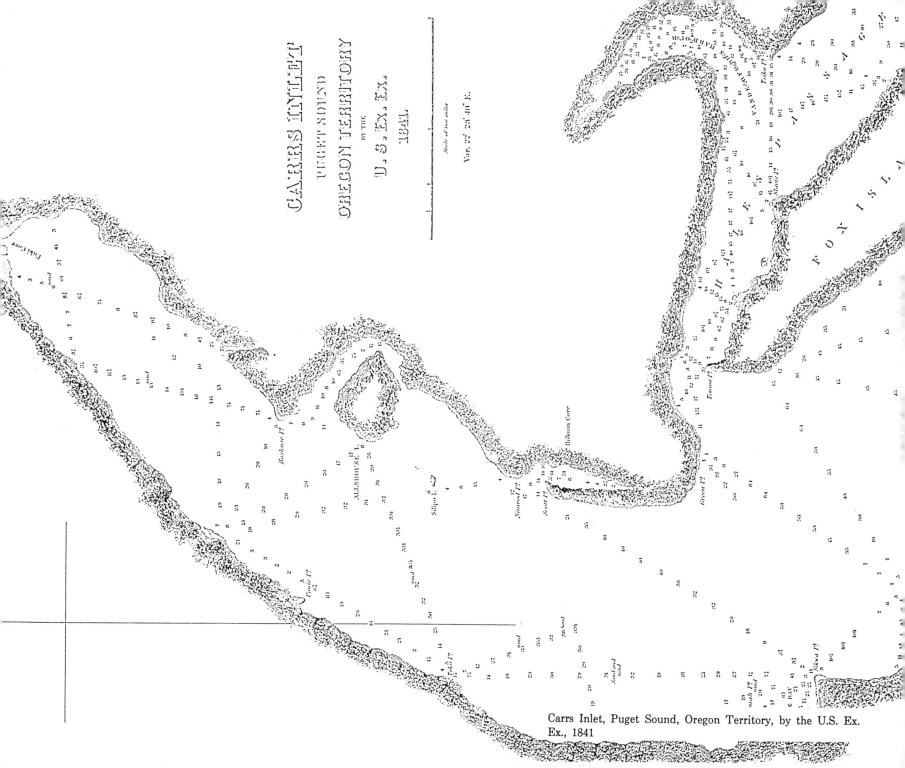

Carrs Inlet, Puget Sound, Oregon Territory, by the U.S. Ex. Ex., 1841

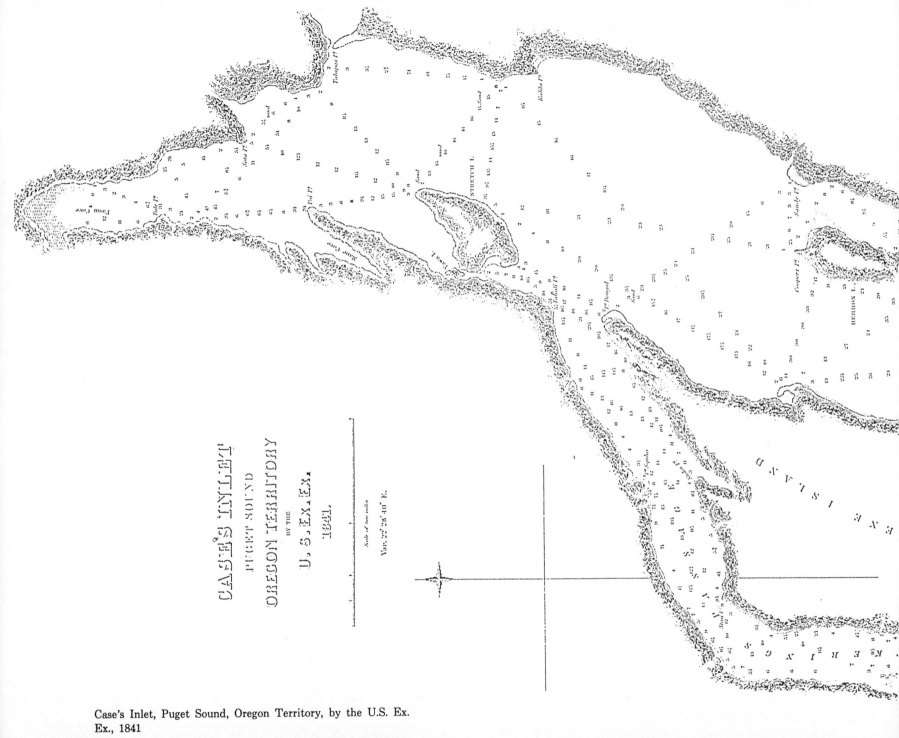

Case's Inlet, Puget Sound, Oregon Territory, by the U.S. Ex.
Ex., 1841

Back to the Pacific

On July 17, Wilkes and his crew departed, leaving behind the Oregon country. On the voyage north, Wilkes took the opportunity to survey areas that had been missed or neglected before, including Whidbey Island, Haro Strait (referred to by Wilkes as Canal de Arro), Hood Canal, and Dungeness. Wilkes' diary is scanty during this period, probably the result of working from dawn to dusk; he made brief notes on the day's activities, but left more detailed observations to less busy times.

On July 27, ten days after the departure from Nisqually, Wilkes received the news he had feared—*Peacock* had been lost on the Columbia River bar. Fortunately, all the crew had been saved, but the ship was a total loss. Wilkes was seriously disturbed by this information; he was eager to question Captain Hudson about the details of the tragedy.

A combination of factors had delayed *Peacock* and *Flying Fish* in the South Seas, and they arrived late at the Columbia River rendezvous. As when Wilkes had arrived, the bar was rough and impassable. However, despite the maelstrom of water, Lieutenant Hudson decided to try his chances at a crossing. After several attempts, he concluded that he had found a clear passage, and proceeded into the waves. The lookout sighted a place where there were no breakers, and the officers were confident they had found the safe channel among the shifting sandbars. Five minutes later the ship touched bottom.

Sachet Stronghold, Whidney's [Whidbey] Island (Joseph Drayton sketch, 1841, Oregon Historical Society, negative number orhi 46195)

Wm L. HUDSON

COMMANDER, U S N

William L. Hudson, Commander, USN

Wreck of the *Peacock* (drawn by A. T. Agate)

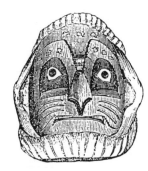

Masks of the Northwest Indians

Hats, Northwest Coast

Hudson immediately sent out a boat to find a clear channel, but none was found. The ship's pumps were put to work in a vain attempt to keep up with the water rushing into the broken hull. All crew were put to work pumping or lightening the load, but the ship pounded on the sand. Eventually, abandonment became inevitable, and the crew took to the boats. Not all were able to get to shore at once, and for a time it was expected that some of the crew would perish aboard the wreck. Fortunately, all were eventually rescued.

The shipwrecked men were welcomed by local residents and provided what assistance the small community of Astoria could give. *Flying Fish* made a successful crossing of the bar, and soon all the Americans were in Astoria, living in a tent village outside the main community. The crew and officers kept busy, but were unable to start a comprehensive survey of the river without proper direction from Wilkes.

Wilkes arrived on August 7, relieved that the crew was safe but angered that the crossing of the bar had gone so badly. He publicly congratulated Hudson for saving the lives of his men, but lamented in his journal that Hudson had not obeyed his orders, thus setting the scene for the wreck.

The Expedition's time in the Oregon country was almost finished. The major project remaining was the survey of the Columbia, which Wilkes began as soon as he arrived at Astoria. A replacement for *Peacock* was purchased, and the men began their work. Wilkes worked his way up the river to Vancouver, where he once again met with the Hudson's Bay Company officials. The survey was completed in early September, and the Expedition once again assembled at Astoria.

Plate 13, Altas to Volume XX, *Herpetology* (Washington
State Library)

"A STATE THAT IS DESTINED TO CONTROL THE DESTINIES OF THE PACIFIC"

by

Frances B. Barkan

The United States Exploring Expedition traveled on to California and then, on their way home, to Hawaii, the Philippines, and Singapore.

After the completion of the Columbia River survey, Wilkes divided his little squadron. Wilkes himself planned to go south to California in the *Porpoise*, while *Flying Fish* was left behind to work her way down the Oregon coast and then sail to Oahu. Some of the crew and officers were ordered to march overland to California. *Vincennes* had already been sent to the port of Yerba Buena, and was awaiting the rest of the squadron's arrival.

Wilkes arrived at San Francisco in the middle of October, and spent part of his time writing a full report on his activities to the Secretary of the Navy. In addition, he made some observations on California and its political situation, promising a more complete verbal report on his return to the nation's capital.

After a short stay in California, Wilkes and his crew left for the Hawaiian Islands, where the entire squadron would rendezvous and reprovision. This stop was the first on their long way home via the Pacific, the Indian Ocean, and, finally, the Atlantic. The ships paused in the Philippines and at Singapore, then sailed for home. On June 10, 1842, the Expedition arrived in the Port of New York, home from four years of the first voyage of exploration sponsored by the American government.

Appichemens

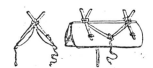

Pack-Saddle

Sack

Parflesh

Map of Upper California, by the U.S. Ex. Ex. and Best
Authorities, 1841

Umpqua Indian Girl

Costume of a Callapuya Indian

The Return Home

The Expedition's arrival in New York started a series of events that would have both personal and professional consequences for Wilkes and his officers. In addition, the Expedition's report on the Oregon country would have a profound effect on the status of the northwest coast.

The Expedition had no sooner anchored than the carefully constructed house of cards fell apart. The dissensions and quarrels festering beneath the polite surface of military discipline erupted almost at once. The Expedition's achievements were put on the shelf and largely ignored. A new administration was in Washington, one uninterested in the Expedition and its achievements. The Congress did not pass a resolution of commendation. Wilkes called on the Secretary of the Navy, and was coldly received, he reported. The Expedition's commander was bitterly disappointed.

Wilkes and his officers filed accusations and counter-charges, pointing reproachful fingers at each other. Junior officers were disrespectful, disobedient, wasteful of government property, and mutinous, according to Wilkes. The accused officers labeled Wilkes oppressive, cruel, and disobedient; in addition, Wilkes was accused of illegally punishing crew members and scandalous conduct. A court martial was appointed to hear the charges, and Wilkes requested that the trials of the junior officers take place first. Wilkes was sure that the court was packed with friends of the Secretary of the Navy, and despaired of getting justice from such an assemblage.

In the event, three of the junior officers were found guilty of various charges.

Wilkes' trial was complicated, taking almost three weeks to complete. Various Expedition officers were called by the prosecution to testify to Wilkes' excitable character, violent manner, and disrespect for his officers and crew. Other officers defended their commander, testifying to Wilkes' devotion to duty. Wilkes made a long statement in his own defense, both explaining his own conduct and accusing his officers of plotting against him and his commands. In his defense, Wilkes stated that he had not asked for the command, but that once he had been given it, he carried out the task to the best of his ability. He admitted that he was concerned about the charges of illegal punishment, but stated that he had acted within Navy Regulations.

The charge of scandalous conduct caught the attention of the public. Wilkes stated that he had seen the Antarctic continent from the deck of the *Vincennes*. Other officers debated the date of the sighting, accusing Wilkes of falsifying his recollections and records. However, Wilkes was supported in his claim by two of the junior officers, who said they had seen indications of land some days before Wilkes claimed to see the seventh continent.

Wilkes was also accused of adopting the trappings of a ship's captain, a rank to which he was not entitled. He answered the charge by noting that he had been given the responsibilities of a captain, and quoted Navy regulations that permitted junior officers to assume the trappings of rank when they received an acting appointment. Additionally, Wilkes pointed out, his actions were nowhere forbidden.

Wilkes vigorously defended himself, and, in the end, he was found guilty of only one charge, that of illegally punishing seamen.

His sentence was light, a public reprimand by the Secretary of the Navy, but it appeared heavy to Wilkes. His reputation, and that of the entire Expedition, suffered as a result of the scandal. Publication of the Expedition's findings became increasingly problematical.

There were no specific provisions made for the Expedition's specimens when the ships left Norfolk in 1838. When they returned, they were stuffed with boxes of exotic animals and plants, rocks and minerals, cultural artifacts and bones from around the globe. In the years after the Expedition returned, more crates, bags, and boxes arrived, carrying more specimens. Some were sent to institutions around the country. The legacy of the Expedition had arrived, and something had to be done with it. In 1835, a bequest had been given to the nation for the establishment of the Smithsonian Institution. Once the bequest was accepted, a process which took some ten years, it appeared that the new organization was the logical place to house the new collection, though for a time other temporary arrangements had to be made. Congress appropriated funds for preservation and the return of portions of the collection from museums in other cities, and the specimens were housed in the Great Hall of the Patent Office.

In time, Charles Wilkes was put in charge of the collection, opening an exhibit to the public and directing the preparation of specimens. The exotic plants collected were cultivated in the nation's Botanical Garden.

Wilkes eventually composed the five volume *Narrative*, telling the Expedition's story to the public. Volumes on scientific discoveries were also planned, and some were published through the 1850's. Other scientific volumes were deferred until after the Civil War. Not all of the publications prepared or planned were actually printed; the last to see the light of day appeared in 1872.

The Expedition left the United States with many legacies, not the least of which was the creation of a national museum of science. American mariners finally could rely on American-made charts of foreign waters. A new continent had been discovered. A tradition of scientific exploration had been started. American scientists created a place for themselves in the world's scientific community. The west coast of the North American continent became firmly entrenched in the national consciousness as part of the national whole. Though the Expedition may have been a failure in human relations, it was a triumph in science and exploration.

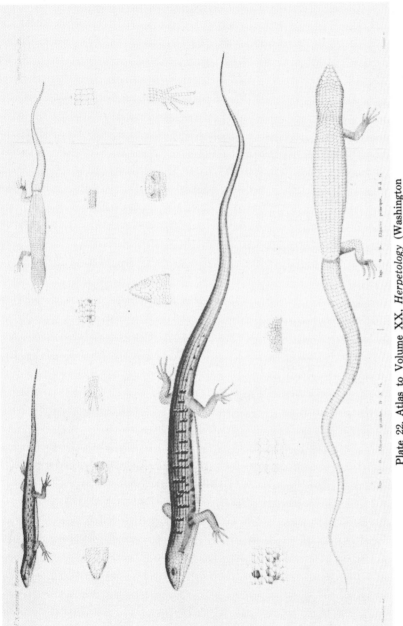

Plate 22, Atlas to Volume XX, *Herpetology* (Washington State Library)

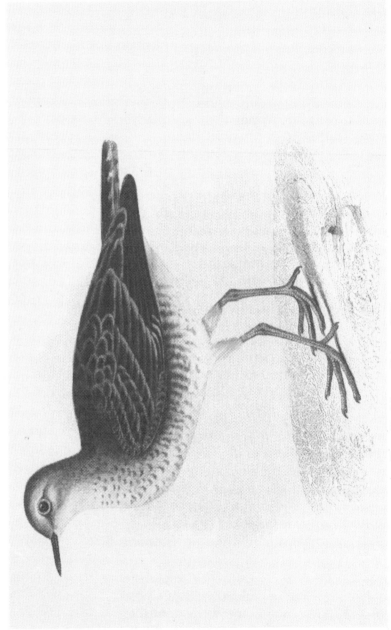

Plate 38, Atlas to Volume VIII
Mammalogy And Ornithology
Special collections Division, University of Washington Libraries

Plate 8, Atlas to Volume VIII, *Mammalogy and Ornithology*
(Special Collections Division, University of Washington
Libraries, negative number UW 5271)

Plate 9, Atlas to Volume VIII, *Mammalogy and Ornithology*
(Special Collections Division, University of Washington
Libraries, negative number UW 5385)

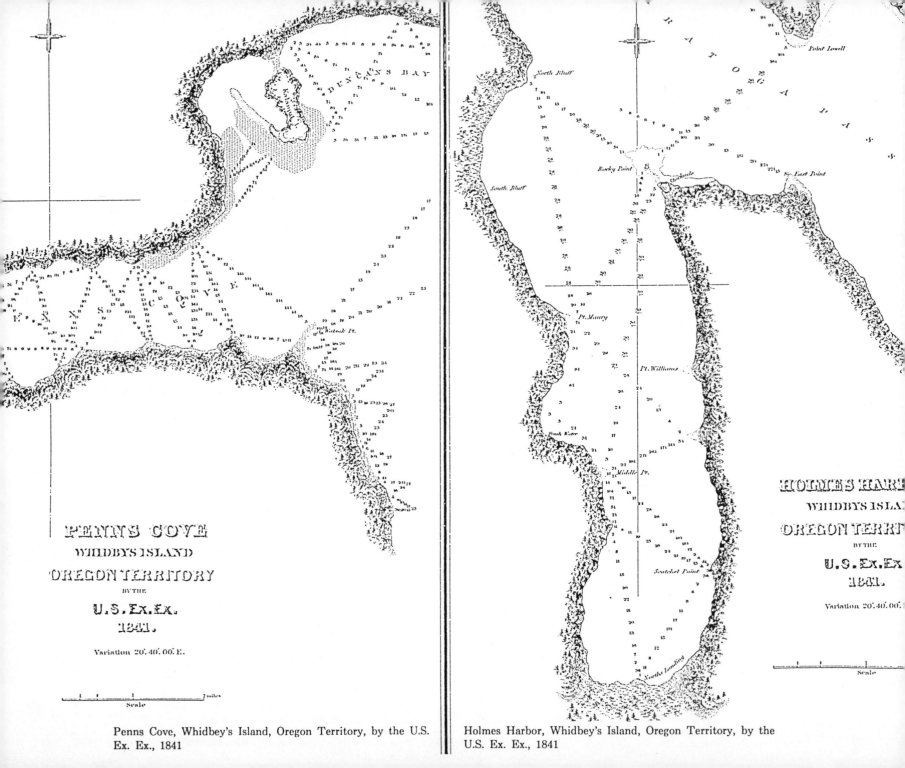

Penns Cove, Whidbey's Island, Oregon Territory, by the U.S. Ex. Ex., 1841

Holmes Harbor, Whidbey's Island, Oregon Territory, by the U.S. Ex. Ex., 1841

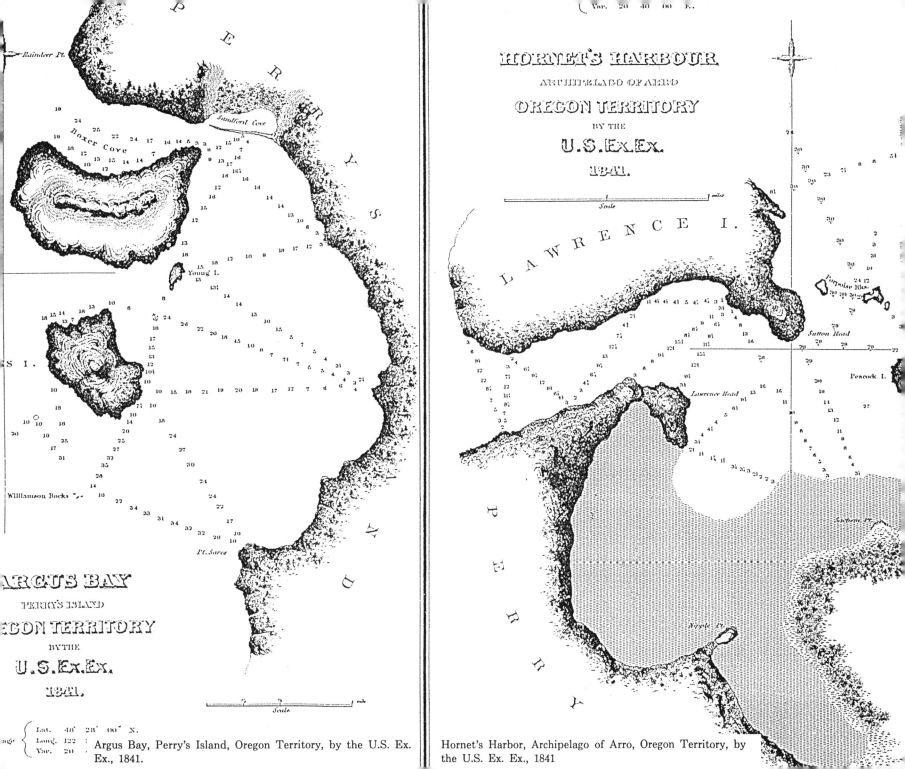

ARGUS BAY

PERRY'S ISLAND

OREGON TERRITORY

BY THE

U.S. Ex. Ex.

1841.

Lat. 48° 28' 00" N.
Long. 122
Var. 20

Argus Bay, Perry's Island, Oregon Territory, by the U.S. Ex. Ex., 1841.

HORNET'S HARBOUR

ARCHIPELAGO OF ARRO

OREGON TERRITORY

BY THE

U.S. Ex. Ex.

1841.

Scale

Hornet's Harbor, Archipelago of Arro, Oregon Territory, by the U.S. Ex. Ex., 1841

The Joint Occupation Treaty

One of the legacies of the Expedition was its contribution to the establishment of the boundary between the United States and Canada, and the addition to the United States of half of the Strait of Juan de Fuca and the inland waters of western Washington. For quite a time, though, the location of the international border was far from certain.

After the War of 1812, the United States and Great Britain signed a joint occupancy treaty. The area on the northwest coast of the North American continent would be free and open to citizens and ships of any nation for ten years after the treaty date of 1818. The border designated in the treaty was the 49th parallel—more or less the present boundary. In 1827, the treaty was extended indefinitely, allowing each nation to annul the treaty on twelve months' notice. Great Britain had requested that the border be made the Columbia River, but the U.S. was able to perpetuate the original boundary agreement.

This situation lingered for some years. At first, there were few American settlements in the area, and the Oregon country, as it became known, was largely occupied by Indians and Hudson's Bay Company trappers and employees. However, American settlers and missionaries began to move into the territory, and there was increased interest in Washington, D. C. regarding the northwest coast. In addition, the Russians, who at that time occupied Alaska, were concerned that neither the British nor the Americans should poach on Russian territory; they proposed a treaty that would set the boundary between Russian and British or American territory at 54 degrees, 40 minutes (the modern Alaska-British Columbia border). Both the British and the Americans were willing to make the agreement, and the northwest coast still fell under the rubric of joint occupation.

With the return of the Wilkes Expedition, and the increased numbers of American settlers, U. S. politicians developed great interest in the Oregon country. James Polk, running for president in 1844, adopted a campaign slogan of "54 40 or fight!" and proposed the annexation of Texas (then an independent nation) and the occupation of Oregon. The British rejected the American claim to the border at 54 degrees, 40 minutes, but expressed some willingness to negotiate after the United States declared it would annul the 1818 joint occupation treaty. A new treaty, the Oregon Treaty of 1846, was drawn up, establishing a boundary at the 49th parallel, giving Vancouver Island to the British and the islands to the south—the San Juans—to the United States. This treaty was ratified in July of 1846.

Because of the tangled and twisted channels and the many islands the borderline crossed, the boundary dispute simmered on, although the major decisions had been made. There were both American and British settlers in the San Juan Islands, and a dispute over a British pig and an American potato patch led these settlers to call for support from their governments in the 1840's. Though soldiers were sent by both nations, no shots were fired, and the pig remained the only casualty. Both nations asked Kaiser Wilhelm to resolve their long-running dispute; in 1872, after a study of the documents, he established the present border.

The States of Oregon and Washington

After Wilkes' visit, Washington and Oregon attracted more and more settlers. Oregon became a United States territory in 1848, and Washington remained as part of the territory until 1853, when it gained territorial status of its own. Oregon became a state in 1859; Washington followed suit in 1889.

Plate 34, Atlas to Volume XII, *Mollusca and Shells* (Washington State Library)

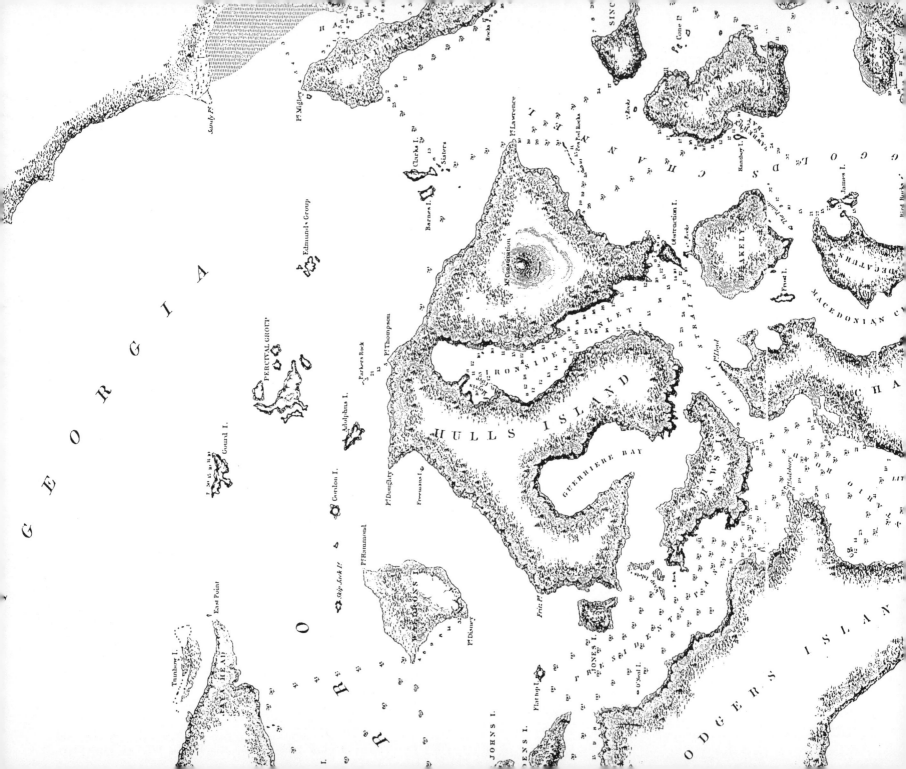

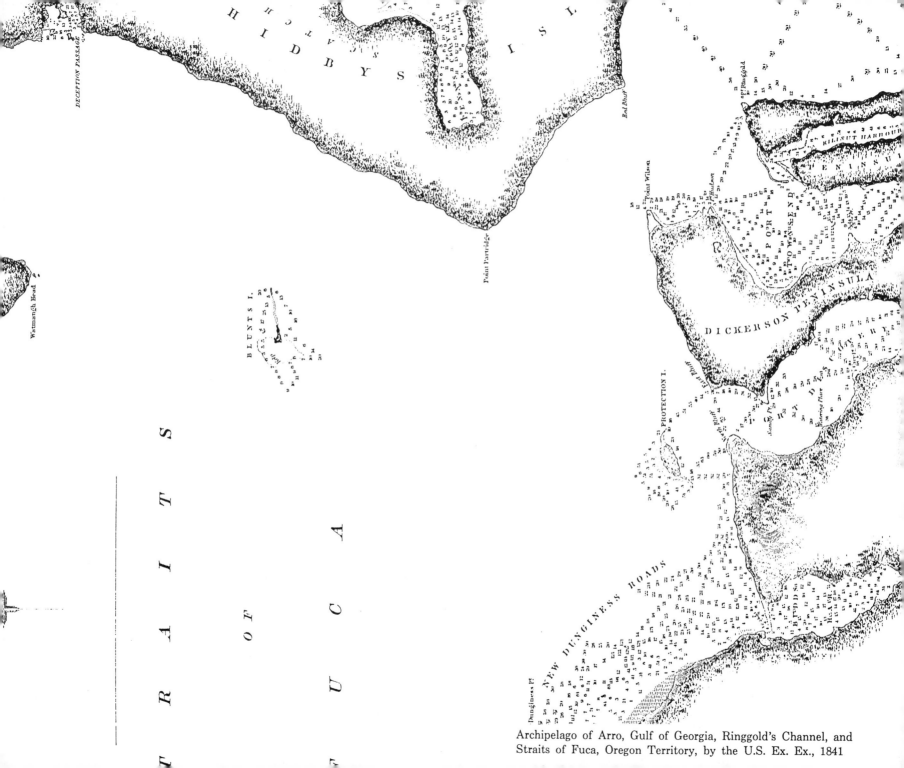

Archipelago of Arro, Gulf of Georgia, Ringgold's Channel, and
Straits of Fuca, Oregon Territory, by the U.S. Ex. Ex., 1841

NAMES ON THE LAND AND WATER

by

Drew Crooks

From the earliest times naming has been a common human activity. People around the world have sought to attach names to parts of their environment, including geographical localities. Individuals who lived in or visited what is now Washington State were no exception. The Wilkes Expedition energetically participated in the naming of features in the area. Many of Wilkes' place names have persisted to the present day, forming a legacy from the 19th century expedition.

The current mosaic of place names in Washington consists of contributions by the Wilkes Expedition and other groups. Before the coming of Wilkes, Native Americans gave place names to the land (e.g., Nahwatzel Lake, Sequalitchew Creek, and Wynoochee River). Eighteenth century Spanish explorers pinned names to their discoveries (e.g., Camano Island, Port Angeles, and San Juan Archipelago), while contemporary English explorers and merchants did the same (e.g.,

Cape Flattery and Mount Olympus). Captain George Vancouver of the British Navy in particular left names in the wake of his voyage (e.g., Mount Rainier, Puget Sound, and Vashon Island). An American merchant, Robert Gray, named the Columbia River. Finally, the employees of the early 19th century fur trading companies, often French Canadian in origin and language, bestowed names on geographical features (e.g., The Dalles, Deschutes River, and Palouse River).

Charles Wilkes, during his visit to the Pacific Northwest, recorded numerous place names. In a number of cases he merely confirmed names previously given by Native Americans or Euro-Americans (e.g., Grand Coulee, Kalamut Island, and Neclim Point). Frequently, however, Wilkes assigned new names. Major sources for the latter were physical descriptions (e.g., Flattop Island, Ostrich Bay, and Rocky Point), men and ships in American naval history—especially the War of 1812 (e.g., Decatur Island, Mount Erie, and Wasp Island), and the Expedition's crew members (e.g., Elliott Bay, Fox Island, and Henderson Inlet).

The naming of geographical localities in the region has naturally continued since the Wilkes Expedition, with increasing standardization imposed by government surveys. The Washington State Board on Geographic Names, in cooperation with the corresponding United States Board, at present oversees nomenclature changes and additions. Many of Wilkes' names remain in use, but surprisingly, no place in Washington is named for the great explorer himself.

Below is a list of names given by the Wilkes Expedition to localities in what is now Washington State. Names which originated with the Expedition are included, while those merely recorded by Wilkes are omitted. When the derivation of a place name is unknown, that fact is noted.

Entries are organized alphabetically, in the following format:

Wilkes name [current name if different] (county)

Source of name if not simply a physical description. Unless otherwise noted, individuals mentioned were expedition crew members.

A second list shows names given by Wilkes by county. The format is as follows:

COUNTY NAME

Name in current use [name given by Wilkes]

References for this chapter were Wilkes Expedition publications, Robert Hitchman's *Place Names of Washington*, and Edmond S. Meany's *Origin of Washington Geographic Names*.

Adolphus Island [non-existent feature] (San Juan County)

Source of name unknown.

Agate Passage (Kitsap County)

Named for Alfred T. Agate, an artist and draftsman assigned to the expedition.

Agate Point (Kitsap County)

Named for Alfred T. Agate.

Ala Spit (Island County)

Source of name unknown.

Allan Island (Skagit County)

"Allan's Island" named for William Henry Allen, a captain in the United States Navy who was mortally wounded in the battle between the *Argus* and the *Pelican* during the War of 1812.

Allhouse Island [Raft Island] (Pierce County)

Named for Joseph Allhouse, a crew member.

Anderson Island (Pierce County)

Named for Alexander Caulfield Anderson of the Hudson's Bay Company, a chief trader at Fort Nisqually.

Annas Bay (Mason County)

Source of name, originally "Anna Bay" or "Anna's Bay", unknown.

Appletree Cove (Kitsap County)

Named for the appearance of flowering apple trees (probably pacific dogwood, *cornus nuttallii*) in the cove.

Ariel Point [Nodule Point] (Jefferson County)

Possibly named for *Ariels*, an American vessel in the War of 1812.

Ariels Point [Double Bluff] (Island County)

Named for *Ariels*, an American vessel in the Battle of Lake Erie during the War of 1812.

Aycock Point (Mason County)

Source of name, originally "Aycock's Point", unknown.

Ayres Point (Mason County)

Named for John Ayres, a crew member.

Bag Island [Brown's Island] (Wahkiakum County)

Bainbridge Island (Kitsap County)

Named for William Bainbridge, a captain in the United States Navy who commanded the *Constitution* in the battle with the *Java* during the War of 1812.

Barnes Island (San Juan County)

Named for an American naval hero from the War of 1812.

Barron's Bay [Yukon Harbor] (Kitsap County)

Named for Samuel Barron, a commodore in the United States Navy who served in the Tripolitan War of 1805.

Bill Point (Kitsap County)

Bird Rock [Sail Rock] (Clallam County)

Bird Rocks (San Juan County)

Blake Island (Kitsap County)

Named for George Smith Blake, an officer in the United States Navy who was in charge of the United States Coast Survey, 1837 to 1848.

Blakely Harbor (Kitsap County)

Named for Johnston Blakely, a captain in the United States Navy who with his ship, the *Wasp*, and crew were lost at sea during the War of 1812.

Blakely Island (San Juan County)

Named for Johnston Blakely, a captain in the United States Navy who with his ship, the *Wasp*, was lost at sea during the War of 1812.

Blunt's Island [Smith Island] (Island County)

Named for Simon F. Blunt, a midshipman.

Bolton Peninsula (Jefferson County)

Source of name uncertain.

Boston Point (Jefferson County)

Named for Boston, Massachusetts.

Boxer Cove [Flounder Bay] (Skagit County)

Named for the *Boxer*, a British vessel captured by the American *Enterprise* during the War of 1812. Lieutenant William Burrows, who commanded the *Enterprise*, died during the fight.

Brackenridge Bluff (Grays Harbor County)

Named for J.D. Brackenridge, an assistant botanist.

Brackenridge Passage [not persisted] (Pierce County)

Named for J.D. Brackenridge, an assistant botanist.

Brisco Point (Mason County)

Named for William Brisco, a crew member.

Brown Island (San Juan County) Probably named for John G. Brown, a mathematical instrument maker.

Brown Island (San Juan County)

Named for an unknown individual.

Brown's Point [Dofflemeyer Point] (Thurston County)

Named for James Brown, a carpenter's mate.

Browns Point (Jefferson County)

Source of name uncertain.

Budd Inlet (Thurston County)

Named for Thomas A. Budd, acting master of the *Peacock* who transferred at Fiji to the *Vincennes*.

Budd's Harbor [Sequim Bay] (Clallam County)

Named for Thomas A. Budd, acting master of the *Peacock*, who transferred at Fiji to the *Vincennes*.

Bull's Head (Jefferson County)

Burrows Bay (Skagit County)

Named for William Burrows, a lieutenant in the United States Navy who was killed in the capture of the *Boxer* during the War of 1812.

Burrows Island (Skagit County)

Named for William Burrows, a lieutenant in the United States Navy who heroically served in the War of 1812.

Bute Prairies [Mound Prairie] (Thurston County)

Commonly known as Mima Mound Prairie.

Carr Inlet (Pierce County)

Named for Overton Carr, a lieutenant.

Carr Point (Jefferson County)

"Carr's Point" named for Overton Carr, a lieutenant.

Case Inlet (Mason and Pierce Counties)

"Case's Inlet" named for A.L. Case, a lieutenant. Sometimes referred to as Cases Inlet.

Case Shoal (Jefferson County)

"Case's Bank" named for A.L. Case, a lieutenant.

Chancy's Island [Lopez Island] (San Juan County)

Named for Isaac Chauncey, a captain in the United States Navy who commanded the *Washington* in 1815 at the battle of Algiers.

Clark Island (San Juan County)

"Clark's Island" named for John Clark, a midshipman in the United States Navy who was killed in the Battle of Lake Erie during the War of 1812.

Clark Point (Skagit County)

"Clark's Point" named for Levin Clark, a captain of the top.

Colvos Passage [West Passage] (King and Kitsap Counties)

Named for George W. Colvocoresses, a passed midshipman.

Colvos Rocks (Jefferson County)

Named for George W. Colvocoresses, a passed midshipman.

Commencement Bay (Pierce County)

Named as starting point for survey of Admiralty Inlet, May, 1841.

Cone Hill [Eagle Cliff] (Skagit County)

Cook Point [Potlatch Point] (Mason County)

Named for John Cook, a boatswain's mate.

Cooper Point (Thurston County)

"Point Cooper" named for John Cooper, an armorer.

Craven Peninsula [Indian Island and Marrowstone Island] (Jefferson County)

Named for Thomas T. Craven, a lieutenant.

Daisy Bluff [base of Kanem Point] (Jefferson County)

Dalco Passage (King and Pierce Counties)

Source of name unknown.

Dana Passage (Mason and Thurston Counties)

"Dana's Passage" named for James Dwight Dana, a mineralogist.

Day Island (Pierce County)

"Days Island" named for Stephen W. Days, a hospital steward.

De Hayens Knoll (Grays Harbor County)

Probably named for E.H. Havens, acting master of the *Flying Fish*, a ship of exploration under the command of Charles Wilkes.

Decatur Island (San Juan County)

"Decatur's Island" named for Stephen Decatur, an officer in the United States Navy who served heroically in the War of 1812 and other conflicts.

Dennis Shoal (Skagit County)

Named for an unidentified crew member.

Dickerson Peninsula [Quimper Peninsula] (Jefferson County)

Named for Mahlon Dickerson, who as Secretary of the Navy in 1838 gave the orders to Charles Wilkes on the United States Exploring Expedition.

Dickerson Point (Thurston County)

Named for Thomas Dickerson, a carpenter's mate.

Dot Island (Skagit County)

Dougall Point (Mason County)

"Dougal Point" named for an unknown individual.

Drayton Harbor (Whatcom County)

"Drayton Bay" named for Joseph Drayton, an artist of the Expedition. Originally the term included the whole of what is now called Semiahmoo Bay.

Drayton Passage (Pierce County)

Named for Joseph Drayton, an artist.

Duncan's Bay [Crescent Harbor] (Island County)

Named for an officer in the United States Navy who during the War of 1812 served on the *Saratoga*.

Dyes Inlet (Kitsap County)

Named for John W. W. Dyes, an assistant taxidermist.

Eagle Harbor (Kitsap County)

Origin of name uncertain. Possible sources include Henry Eagle, a contemporary lieutenant in the United States Navy; the *Eagle*, ship of War in the War of 1812; the shape of the geographical feature; or the presence of eagles in the area.

East Point (Island County)

Point is located on Whidbey Island's eastern shore.

Edmunds Group [Matia and Puffin Islands] (San Juan County)

Named for an unidentified crew member.

Eld Inlet (Mason and Thurston Counties)

Named for Henry Eld, a passed midshipman. Mud Bay is a local name for the inlet.

Eld's Island [locality destroyed by jetty construction or dredging] (Grays Harbor County)

Named for Henry Eld, a passed midshipman.

Eliza Island (Whatcom County)

"Eliza's Island" named for Lieutenant Juan Francisco de Eliza, a Spanish explorer who in 1791 explored the same area.

Elliott Bay (King County)

Named for Samuel Elliott, a midshipman.

Flag Point [Walan Point] (Jefferson County)

Flattop Island (San Juan County)

Name believed to depict the topographical shape of the island.

Fox Island (Pierce County)

Named for J.L. Fox, an assistant surgeon.

Freeman Island (San Juan County)

"Freeman's Island" named for J.D. Freeman, a sailmaker.

Fritz Point (San Juan County)

Source of name unknown.

Frolic Strait [Upright Channel] (San Juan County)

Named for the *Frolic*, a British brigantine captured by the *Wasp* during the War of 1812.

Frost Island (San Juan County)

Named for John Frost, a boatswain.

Gedney Island (Snohomish County)

Possibly named for Jonathan Haight Gedney, a New York inventor.

Geese Islets [Group name not persisted, replaced by individual names including Long Island, Buck Island, Mummy Rocks, and Whale Rocks] (San Juan County)

Gibson Point (Pierce County)

"Point Gibson" named for James H. Gibson, a coxswain.

Gig Harbor (Pierce County)

Descriptive name given to indicate a depth sufficient only for small vessels to enter.

Gordon Island [non-existent feature] (San Juan County)

Source of name unknown.

Gordon Point [Restoration Point] (Kitsap County)

Named for John Gordon, a quartermaster on the expedition.

Gourd Island [Patos Island] (San Juan County)

Grays Point (Pacific County)

Named for Robert Gray, the American captain who discovered the Columbia River, 1792.

Green Point (Pierce County)

Named for Daniel Green, a gunner's mate.

Guerriere Bay [West Sound] (San Juan County)

Named for a British frigate, the *Guerriere*, captured by the American *Constitution* during the War of 1812.

Hale Passage (Whatcom County)

Named for Horatio Hale, a philologist and ethnographer.

Hale Passage (Pierce County)

Named for Horatio Hale, a philologist and ethnographer.

Hammersley Inlet (Mason County)

Named for George W. Hammersly, a midshipman.

Hartstene Island (Mason County)

Named for Henry J. Hartstene, a lieutenant.

Hautboy Island [Strawberry Island] (Skagit County)

Named for hautboy, the common name for a species of strawberry, "Fragaria elatior".

Helix Point [Mill Point] (Jefferson County)

Henderson Inlet (Thurston County)

Named for James Henderson, a quartermaster. South Bay is a local name for the inlet.

Henry Island (San Juan County)

Named for Wilkes Henry, a midshipman of the expedition who was killed in July 1840 by natives of the Fiji Islands. Wilkes Henry was a nephew of Charles Wilkes.

Herron Island (Pierce County)

Named for Lewis Herron, a petty officer.

Holmes Harbor (Island County)

Named for Silas Holmes, an assistant surgeon.

Hope Island (Mason County)

Source of name unknown.

Hope Island (Skagit County)

Source of name unknown.

Hornet's Harbor [Guemes Channel] (Skagit County)

Named for the *Hornet*, an American ship which saw action under Captain James Lawrence during the War of 1812.

Hoypus Point (Island County)

Source of name, originally "Hoipus Point," unknown.

Hudson Point (Jefferson County)

"Hudson's Point" named for William F. Hudson, commander of the *Peacock*.

Hulls Island [Orcas Island] (San Juan County)

Named for Isaac Hull, a commodore in the United States Navy who commanded the *Constitution* during the War of 1812.

Hyde Point (Pierce County)

Named for William Hyde, a carpenter's mate.

Indian (or Great) Peninsula (Kitsap, Mason and Pierce Counties)

No longer designated. Generally the peninsula between the Hood Canal and Puget Sound.

Indian Point (Island County)

Ironsides Inlet [East Sound] (San Juan County)

Named for "Old Ironsides," the nickname of the *Constitution*, a famous American frigate of the War of 1812.

Itsami Ledge (Thurston County)

Source of name unknown.

Jack Island (Skagit County)

Perhaps named for jack, a common name for a sailor.

Jack's Island [Squaxin Island] (Mason County)

Perhaps named for jack, a common name for a sailor.

James Island (San Juan County)

Possibly named for Reuben James, an American sailor who in the Tripoli campaign saved the life of Stephen Decatur.

Joe's Bank (Grays Harbor County)

Named for Joe, a mixed blood interpreter.

Johns Island (San Juan County)

Named for an unknown sailor.

Jones Island (San Juan County)

Named for Jacob Jones, a captain in the United States Navy who, as master commandant of the *Wasp*, captured the *Frolic* during the War of 1812.

Jupiter Hills (Jefferson County)

Named for the Roman god.

Kellum's Lake Isthmus (Mason County)

Named for John Kellum, a quartermaster.

Kellum's Lake [Mason Lake] (Mason County)

Named for John Kellum, a quartermaster.

Ketron Island (Pierce County)

Named, but misspelled, for William Kittson of the Hudson's Bay Company.

Lawrence Island [Guemes Island] (Skagit County)

Named for James Lawrence, a captain in the United States Navy who died in the battle between the *Chesapeake* and the *Shannon* during the War of 1812.

Lawrence Point (San Juan County)

"Point Lawrence" named for James Lawrence, a captain in the United States Navy who died in the battle between the *Chesapeake* and the *Shannon* during the War of 1812.

Levant Passage (Skagit County)

Named for the *Levant*, a British ship captured by the *Constitution* during the War of 1812.

Little Belt Passage [Middle Channel] (San Juan County)

Named for the *Little Belt*, a British ship fought by Commodore John Rodgers of the United States in 1811.

Loa Point [Nisqually Head] (Thurston County)

Probably named for Mauna Loa, Hawaii.

Lynch Cove (Mason County)

Named for William Francis Lynch, a lieutenant in the United States Navy who explored the Dead Sea and the Jordan River.

Macedonian Crescent [Lopez Sound and Thatcher Pass] (San Juan County)

Named for the *Macedonian*, a British vessel captured by Captain Decatur of the United States Navy during the War of 1812.

Manhait Point (Pierce County)

Source of name unknown.

Maury Island (King County)

Named for William L. Maury, a lieutenant who served as an astronomer and hydrographer. A sand spit connects this "island" to Vashon Island.

May's Inlet [Liberty Bay] (Kitsap County)

Named for William May, a passed midshipman.

McDonough's Island [Camano Island] (Island County)

Named for Thomas MacDonough, a master commandant in the United States Navy who led the *Saratoga* to victory in the battle of Lake Champlain during the War of 1812.

McLaughlin's Island [Lummi Island] (Whatcom County)

Named for Dr. John McLoughlin, the Chief Factor at Fort Vancouver, who greatly helped the Wilkes Expedition.

McNeil Island (Pierce County)

Named for William Henry McNeill of the Hudson's Bay Company, who was captain of the *Beaver*.

Mount Constitution (San Juan County)

Named for the *Constitution*, a famous American frigate of the War of 1812.

Mount Erie (Skagit County)

Named for the Battle of Lake Erie, won by Commodore Oliver Hazard Perry during the War of 1812.

Mount St. Pierre [Badger Mountain] (Douglas County)

Perhaps named for Pierre Charles, a retired Hudson's Bay Company employee. Charles guided Lieutenant Robert Johnson and his party overland through present day Eastern Washington.

The Narrows (Pierce County)

Originally named "Narrows."

Navy Archipelago [San Juan Archipelago] (San Juan County)

Named for the United States Navy.

Neds Rock (Grays Harbor County)

Source of name unknown.

Neill Point (King County)

Named for William Neill, a quartermaster.

Nequamos Island [Reservation Head] (Skagit County)

Source of name unknown.

North Bluff (Island County)

Named for James North, acting master of the *Vincennes*.

North Bluff [Diamond Point] (Clallam County)

Nut Islets [Dago and Squaw Island] (Clark County)

Source of name unknown.

O'Neal Island (San Juan County)

Named for an American naval hero of the War of 1812.

Obstruction Island (San Juan County)

Ontario Roads [Griffin Bay and part of San Juan Channel] (San Juan County)

Named for Lake Ontario where Captain Isaac Chauncey of the United States Navy served during the War of 1812.

Oro Bay (Pierce County)

Source of name unknown.

Ostrich Bay (Kitsap County)

The geographical feature appeared to the explorers to be shaped like an ostrich.

Park Point [Devil's Head] (Pierce County)

Named for David P. Park, a sailmaker's mate.

Parker Reef (San Juan County)

"Parker's Rock" named for George Parker, a petty officer.

Paun Cove [North Bay] (Mason County)

Source of name unknown.

Peacock Island [Hat Island] (Skagit County)

Named for the *Peacock*.

Peacock Spit (Pacific County)

Named for the *Peacock*, which was wrecked here in July, 1841.

Peale Passage (Mason County)

"Peale's Passage" named for Titian R. Peale, a naturalist.

Peapod Rocks (San Juan County)

Pearl Island (San Juan County)

Penguin Harbor [incorporated into Bellingham Channel] (Skagit County)

Named for the *Penguin*, a British ship captured by Captain James Lawrence and the *Hornet* during the War of 1812.

Percival Group [Sucia Islands] (San Juan County)

Named for John Percival, a distinguished captain in the United States Navy.

Perry's Island [Fidalgo Island] (Skagit County)

Named for Oliver Hazard Perry, a commodore in the United States Navy who was victorious in the Battle of Lake Erie during the War of 1812.

Pickering Passage (Mason County)

Named for Charles Pickering, a naturalist.

Pilots Cove (Kitsap County)

Named for meeting in May, 1841 with the first officer of the *Beaver*, a Hudson's Bay Company steamer, who served Wilkes as pilot to Fort Nisqually.

Pitship Point (Clallam County)

Named for an unidentified crew member.

Pitt Island (Pierce County)

Source of name for "Pit Island" unknown.

Plomondon Island [Fisher Island] (Cowlitz County)

Named for Simon Plomondon, or Plamondon, a retired Hudson's Bay employee who served as a guide for Wilkes during his overland trip to Fort Vancouver.

Point Beals (King County)

Named for Artimeus W. Beals, a captain of the hold.

Point Bolin (Kitsap County)

Named for Jacob Bolin, a captain of the forecastle.

Point Carter (Whatcom County)

Named for William Carter, a captain of the top.

Point Crowlie (Mason County)

Named for Charles E. Crowley, a lieutenant in the United States Navy who was noted for heroism in the Battle of New Orleans during the War of 1812.

Point Cummings (Mason County)

Named for W.H. Cummings, a boatswain's mate.

Point Dalco (King County)

Source of name unknown.

Point Defiance (Pierce County)

Named, to note, as Wilkes wrote in *Western America* (page 81), that "This narrow pass [The Narrows] seems as if intended by nature to afford every means for the defense of Puget's Sound,... the only entrance to which is through the narrows, which, if strongly fortified, would bid defiance to any attack and guard its entrance against any force".

Point Demock (Island County)

Named for John Demock, a captain of the top.

Point Disney (San Juan County)

Named for Solomon Disney, a sailmaker's mate.

Point Doughty (San Juan County)

Named for John Doughty, a captain of the top.

Point Edmund [Point Edwards] (Snohomish County)

Source of name unknown.

Point Elliot (Snohomish County)

Named for Samuel Elliot, a midshipman.

Point Fosdick (Pierce County)

Named for Stephen Fosdick, a gunner's mate.

Point Glover (Kitsap County)

Named for John Glover, a captain of the top.

Point Hammond (San Juan County)

Named for Henry Hammond, a quartermaster.

Point Hannon (Jefferson County)

Named for an unidentified crew member.

Point Harmon (Pierce County)

Named for John Harmon, a captain of the forecastle.

Point Harris [Browns Point] (Pierce County)

Named for Alvin Harris, a sailmaker's mate.

Point Herron (Kitsap County)

Named for Lewis Herron, a cooper.

Point Heyer (King County)

"Hyer's Point" named for Henry R. Heyer, a quartermaster of the Wilkes crew.

Point Hilcomb [Koitlah Point] (Clallam County)

Point Jefferson (Kitsap County)

Named for Thomas Jefferson, the third president of the United States.

Point Julia (Kitsap County)

Source of name unknown.

Point Leavett [Bush Point] (Island County)

Named for an unknown crew member.

Point Lloyd [Upright Head] (San Juan County)

Named for William Lloyd, a captain of the top.

Point Lowell (Island County)

Named for James Lowell, a captain of the forecastle.

Point Madison Bay (Kitsap County)

Named for James Madison, the fourth president of the United States.

Point Migley [Priest Point] (Snohomish County)

Named for William Migley, a quarter gunner.

Point Migley (Whatcom County)

Named for William Migley, a quarter gunner.

Point Monroe (Kitsap County)

Named for James Monroe, the fifth president of the United States.

Point Moody [Johnson Point] (Thurston County)

Named for William Moody, a quartermaster.

Point No Point (Kitsap County)

Named for the general appearance of the land formation—low, and not obvious until quite close.

Point Piner (King County)

Named for Thomas Piner, a quartermaster

Point Polnell (Island County)

Named for John Polnell, a quarter gunner.

Point Pulley (King County)

Named for Robert Pulley, a quartermaster.

Point Richmond (Pierce County)

Named for William Richmond, a boatswain's mate.

Point Ringgold [Marrowstone Point] (Jefferson County)

Named for Cadwalader Ringgold, a lieutenant.

Point Roberts [Alki Point] (King County)

Name for an unidentified individual.

Point Salsbury [Turn Island] (San Juan County)

Named for Francis Salsbury, a captain of the top.

Point Sares [Langley Point] (Skagit County)

Named for Henry Sares, a captain of the top. Later a cliff, one mile south, was called "Sares Head".

Point Southworth (Kitsap County)

Named for Edward Southworth, a quartermaster.

Point Thompson (San Juan County)

Named for Matthew Thompson, a captain of the top.

Point Totten [Port Gamble (town)] (Kitsap County)

Named for George M. Totten, a passed midshipman.

Point Treble (Pierce County)

Named for George Treble, a seaman.

Point Turner (Kitsap County)

Named for Henry Turner, a captain of the forecastle.

Point Wells (Snohomish County)

Named for William Wells, a yeoman.

Point White (Kitsap County)

Named for James White, a captain of the forecastle.

Point Whitehorn (Whatcom County)

Named for Daniel Whitehorn, a quarter gunner.

Point Williams (King County)

"William's Point" named for Samuel Williams, a gunner's mate.

The Pointers (San Juan County)

Porpoise Rocks [Dot, Huckleberry, and Saddlebag Islands] (Skagit County)

Probably named for the *Porpoise*.

Port Gamble [Bay] (Kitsap County)

Named for Robert Gamble, a lieutenant in the United Sates Navy who died in the battle between the *President* and the *Belvidere* during the War of 1812.

Port Lawrence [Oak Bay] (Jefferson County)

Named for James Lawrence, a captain in the United States Navy who died in the battle between the *Chesapeake* and the *Shannon* during the War of 1812.

Port Ludlow (Jefferson County)

Named for Augustus C. Ludlow, a lieutenant in the United States Navy who died on the *Chesapeake* in the battle with the *Shannon* during the War of 1812.

President Channel [San Juan Channel] (San Juan County)

Named for the *President*, an American ship which under the command of Commodore John Rodgers battled the *Little Belt* in 1811.

Quartermaster Cove [Smith Cove] (King County)

Rationale for name unknown.

Quartermaster Harbor (King County)

Named, whimsically, as a haven for petty officers' spirits.

Red Bluff [Admiralty Head] (Island County)

Rich Passage (Kitsap County)

"Rich's Passage" named for William Rich, a botanist.

Ringgold's Channel [Rosario Strait] (Island, San Juan, Skagit and Whatcom Counties)

Named for Cadwalader Ringgold, a lieutenant.

Ringgold's Channel [Rosario Strait] (San Juan County)

Named for Cadwalader Ringgold, a lieutenant.

Robinson Point (King County)

"Point Robinson" named for John Robinson, a captain of the forecastle.

Rocky Point (Island County)

Rodgers Island [San Juan Island] (San Juan County)

Named for John Rodgers, a commodore in the United States Navy who commanded the *President* in the battle with the *Little Belt* in 1811.

Rogers Creek [O'Leary Creek] (Grays Harbor County)

Named for one of the expedition's marines.

Sachem Point [March Point] (Skagit County)

Rationale for name unknown.

Sail Rock [Seal Rock] (Clallam County)

Sail Rock Point [Klachopis Point] (Clallam County)

Saint Helens Reach (Wahkiakum County)

Named for Mount Saint Helens.

Salom Point (Mason County)

Source of name unknown.

Salsbury Point (Kitsap County)

Named for Francis Salsbury, a captain of the top.

Samego Point (Pierce County)

Source of name unknown.

Sandford Cove [Flounder Bay] (Skagit County)

Named for Thomas Sandford, a quartermaster.

Sandford Point (King County)

"Point Sandford" named for Thomas Sandford, a quartermaster.

Sandy Point [Beckett Point] (Jefferson County)

Named for the geological feature.

Sandy Point (Thurston County)

Sandy Point (Whatcom County)

Sandy Point (Island County)

Sandy Point [Hood Point] (Kitsap County)

Saratoga Passage (Island County)

Named for the *Saratoga*, the American flagship commanded by Thomas MacDonough in the Battle of Lake Champlain during the War of 1812.

Scarborough Harbor [Neah Bay] (Clallam County)

Named for Captain James Scarborough, of the Hudson's Bay Company, who assisted the Wilkes Expedition.

Scott Island [Cutts Island] (Pierce County)

Named for Thomas Scott, a quartermaster.

Scott Point (Pierce County)

Named for Thomas Scott, a quartermaster.

Sentinel Island (San Juan County)

Shaw Island (San Juan County)

"Shaw's Island" named for John D. Shaw, a captain in the United States Navy who fought prominently in the War of 1812 and the 1815 war against Algiers.

Ship Jack Islands [Bare and Skipjack Islands] (Skagit County) Possibly named for fish, of which several species are commonly called "shipjack".

Sinclair Inlet (Kitsap County)

Named for George T. Sinclair, an acting master.

Sinclair Island (Skagit County)

Probably named for Arthur Sinclair, Sr., a captain in the United States Navy who commanded the *Argus* during the War of 1812.

Sisters (Jefferson County)

Originally called "The Sisters" by Charles Wilkes.

The Sisters (San Juan County)

Originally called "Sisters" by Wilkes.

Sisters Point (Mason County)

Smoke Island [Martin Island] (Cowlitz County)

Sopun Inlet (Grays Harbor County)

Source of name unknown.

Spak Point (Clallam County)

Source of name unknown

Spar Point (Grays Harbor County)

Spieden Bluff (San Juan County)

Named for William Spieden, a purser.

Stretch Island (Mason County)

Named for Samuel Stretch, a gunner's mate.

Stuart Island (San Juan County)

Named for Fredrick D. Stuart, a captain's clerk.

Stuzi Island [Jackson's Island] (Wahkiakum County)

Source of name unknown.

Tatsolo Point (Pierce County)

Source of name unknown.

Termination Point (Jefferson County)

Point is located at the north termination, or end, of Hood Canal.

Toliva Shoal (Pierce County)

Source of name unknown.

Tongue Point [Semiahmoo] (Whatcom County)

Totten Inlet (Mason and Thurston Counties)

Named for George M. Totten, a midshipman. Oyster Bay is a local name for the inlet.

Traitors Inlet (Grays Harbor County)

Named for time, in July and August 1841, when hired Indians refused to assist survey parties and made threats of violence.

Triton Head (Mason County)

Probably named for Triton, a Greek god of the sea.

Typha Creek [Stafford Creek] (Grays Harbor County)

Source of name unknown.

Useless Bay (Island County)

Shallow and exposed to storms, the bay appeared useless to the Wilkes Expedition.

Useless Bay [North Bay] (Grays Harbor County)

Bay was considered of little value by Wilkes Expedition because of its shallow nature, winding channels, and sand bars.

Vanderford's Harbor [Wollochet Bay] (Pierce County)

Named for Benjamin Vanderford, pilot of the *Vincennes*.

Vashon Point (King County)

"Vashon's Point" named for Vashon Island.

Vendovi Island (Skagit County)

Named for Vendovi, a chief from the Fiji Islands who was taken prisoner by Charles Wilkes and afterwards accompanied the explorers during their travels.

Village Point (Whatcom County)

Village Point [Baada Point] (Clallam County)

Source of name depicted the location of a village.

Violet Point (Jefferson County)

Viti Rocks (Whatcom County)

Named for the Viti, or Fiji Islands, home of the prisoner Vendovi.

Waldron Island (San Juan County)

Probably named for Thomas W. Waldron, a captain's clerk. R.R. Waldron, a purser, might also have been honored.

Wasp Islands [Group name still used; individual names also used, including Cliff, Coon, Low, McConnell, Nob, Reef and Yellow Islands, and Bird (or Cormorant) Rock] (San Juan County)

Named for the *Wasp*, an American ship commanded by Commodore Jacob Jones, which captured the *Frolic* during the War of 1812.

Watmough Head (San Juan County)

Named for John Goddard Watmough, a lieutenant in the United States Army who was wounded at Fort Erie during the War of 1812.

West Point (King County)

Williamson Rocks (Skagit County)

Named for John G. Williamson, a gunner.

Wilson Point (Mason County)

Named for Thomas Wilson, a sailmaker's mate.

Wing Point (Kitsap County)

Yoman Point (Pierce County)

Source of name unknown.

Young Island (Skagit County)

"Young's Island" probably named for Ewing Young, an Oregon pioneer.

CLALLAM COUNTY

Baada Point [Village Point]

Diamond Point [North Bluff]

Klachopis Point [Sail Rock Point]

Koitlah Point [Point Hilcomb]

Neah Bay [Scarborough Harbor]

Pitship Point

Sail Rock [Bird Rock]

Seal Rock [Sail Rock]

Sequim Bay [Budd's Harbor]

Spak Point

CLARK COUNTY

Dago and Squaw Island [Nut Islets]

COWLITZ COUNTY

Fisher Island [Plomondon Island]

Martin Island [Smoke Island]

DOUGLAS COUNTY

Badger Mountain [Mount St. Pierre]

GRAYS HARBOR COUNTY

Brackenridge Bluff

De Hayens Knoll

locality destroyed by jetty construction or dredging [Eld's Island]

Joe's Bank

Neds Rock

North Bay [Useless Bay]

O'Leary Creek [Rogers Creek]

Sopun Inlet

Spar Point

Traitors Inlet

ISLAND COUNTY

Admiralty Head [Red Bluff]

Ala Spit

Bush Point [Point Leavett]

Camano Island [McDonough's Island]

Crescent Harbor [Duncan's Bay]

Double Bluff [Ariels Point]

East Point

Holmes Harbor

Hoypus Point

Indian Point

North Bluff

Point Demock

Point Lowell

Point Polnell

Rocky Point

Rosario Strait [Ringgold's Channel]

Sandy Point

Saratoga Passage

Smith Island [Blunt's Island]

Useless Bay

JEFFERSON COUNTY

Beckett Point [Sandy Point]

Bolton Peninsula

Boston Point

Browns Point

Bull's Head

Carr Point

Case Shoal

Colvos Rocks

Hudson Point

Indian Island and Marrowstone Island [Craven Peninsula]

Jupiter Hills

base of Kanem Point [Daisy Bluff]

Marrowstone Point [Point Ringgold]

Mill Point [Helix Point]

Nodule Point [Ariel Point]

Oak Bay [Port Lawrence]

Point Hannon

Port Ludlow

Quimper Peninsula [Dickerson Peninsula]

Sisters

Termination Point

Violet Point

Walan Point [Flag Point]

KING COUNTY

Alki Point [Point Roberts]
Dalco Passage
Elliott Bay
Maury Island
Neill Point
Point Beals
Point Dalco
Point Heyer
Point Piner
Point Pulley
Point Williams
Quartermaster Harbor
Robinson Point
Sandford Point
Smith Cove [Quartermaster Cove]
Vashon Point
West Passage [Colvos Passage]
West Point

KITSAP COUNTY

Agate Passage
Agate Point
Appletree Cove
Bainbridge Island
Bill Point

Blake Island
Blakely Harbor
Dyes Inlet
Eagle Harbor
Hood Point [Sandy Point]
Indian (or Great) Peninsula
Liberty Bay [May's Inlet]
Ostrich Bay
Pilots Cove
Point Bolin
Point Glover
Point Herron
Point Jefferson
Point Julia
Port Gamble Bay
Port Gamble (town) [Point Totten]
Point Madison Bay
Point Monroe
Point No Point
Point Southworth
Point Turner
Point White
Restoration Point [Gordon Point]
Rich Passage
Salsbury Point
Sinclair Inlet
West Passage [Colvos Passage]
Wing Point
Yukon Harbor [Barron's Bay]

MASON COUNTY

Annas Bay
Aycock Point
Ayres Point
Brisco Point
Case Inlet
Dana Passage
Dougall Point
Eld Inlet
Hammersley Inlet
Harstene Island
Hope Island
Indian (or Great) Peninsula
Kellum's Lake Isthmus
Lynch Cove
Mason Lake [Kellum's Lake]
North Bay [Paun Cove]
Peale Passage
Pickering Passage
Point Crowlie
Point Cummings
Potlatch Point [Cook Point]
Salom Point
Sisters Point
Stretch Island
Squaxin Island [Jack's Island]
Totten Inlet
Triton Head
Wilson Point

PACIFIC COUNTY

Grays Point
Peacock Spit

PIERCE COUNTY

Anderson Island
not persisted [Brackenridge Passage]
Browns Point [Point Harris]
Carr Inlet
Case Inlet
Commencement Bay
Cutts Island [Scott Island]
Dalco Pasage
Day Island
Devil's Head [Park Point]
Drayton Passage
Fox Island
Gibson Point
Gig Harbor
Green Point
Hale Passage
Herron Island
Hyde Point
Indian (or Great) Peninsula
Ketron Island

Manhait Point

McNeil Island

Oro Bay

Pitt Island

Point Defiance

Point Fosdick

Point Harmon

Point Richmond

Point Treble

Raft Island [Allhouse Island]

Samego Point

Scott Point

Tatsolo Point

The Narrows

Toliva Shoal

Wollochet Bay [Vanderford's Harbor]

Yoman Point

SAN JUAN COUNTY

non-existent feature [Adolphus Island]

Barnes Island

Bird Rocks

Blakely Island

Brown Island

Clark Island

Decatur Island

East Sound [Ironsides Inlet]

Flattop Island

Freeman Island

Fritz Point

Frost Island

non-existent feature [Gordon Island]

Griffin Bay and part of San Juan Channel
[Ontario Roads]

Group name not persisted, replaced by
individual names including Long Island, Buck
Island, Mummy Rocks, and Whale Rocks
[Geese Islets]

Henry Island

James Island

Johns Island

Jones Island

Lawrence Point

Lopez Island [Chancy's Island]

Lopez Sound and Thatcher Pass [Macedonian
Crescent]

Matia and Puffin Islands [Edmunds Group]

Middle Channel [Little Belt Passage]

Mount Constitution

O'Neal Island

Obstruction Island

Orcas Island [Hulls Island]

Parker Reef

Patos Island [Gourd Island]

Peapod Rocks

Pearl Island

Point Disney

Point Doughty

Point Hammond

Point Thompson

Rosario Strait [Ringgold's Channel]

San Juan Archipelago [Navy Archipelago]

San Juan Channel [President Channel]

San Juan Island [Rodgers Island]

Sentinel Island

Sentinel Rock

Shaw Island

Spieden Bluff

Stuart Island

Sucia Islands [Percival Group]

The Pointers

The Sisters

Turn Island [Point Salsbury]

Upright Channel [Frolic Strait]

Upright Head [Point Lloyd]

Waldron Island

Wasp Islands (Group name still used, but individual names given to islands, including Cliff, Coon, Low, McConnell, Nob, Reef and Yellow Islands, and Bird [or Cormorant] Rock)

Watmough Head

West Sound [Guerriere Bay]

SKAGIT COUNTY

Allan Island

Bare and Skipjack Islands [Ship Jack Islands]

incorporated into Bellingham Channel [Penguin Harbor]

Burrows Bay

Burrows Island

Clark Point

Dennis Shoal

Dot, Huckleberry, and Saddlebag Islands [Porpoise Rocks]

Dot Island

Eagle Cliff [Cone Hill]

Fidalgo Island [Perry's Island]

Flounder Bay [Boxer Cove]

Flounder Bay [Sandford Cove]

Guemes Channel [Hornet's Harbor]

Guemes Island [Laurence Island]

Hat Island [Peacock Island]

Hope Island

Jack Island

Langley Point [Point Sares]

Levant Passage

March Point [Sachem Point]

Mount Erie

Reservation Head [Neguamos Island]

Rosario Strait [Ringgold's Channel]

Sinclair Island

Strawberry Island [Hautboy Island]

Vendovi Island

Williamson Rocks

Young Island

SNOHOMISH COUNTY

Gedney Island

Point Edwards [Point Edmund]

Point Elliot

Point Wells

Priest Point [Point Migley]

THURSTON COUNTY

Budd Inlet

Cooper Point

Dana Passage

Dickerson Point

Dofflemeyer Point [Brown's Point]

Eld Inlet

Henderson Inlet

Itsami Ledge

Johnson Point [Point Moody]

Mound Prairie [Bute Prairies]

Nisqually Head [Loa Point]

Sandy Point

Totten Inlet

WAHKIAKUM COUNTY

Brown's Island [Bag Island]

Jackson's Island [Stuzi Island]

Saint Helens Reach

WHATCOM COUNTY

Drayton Harbor

Eliza Island

Hale Passage

Lummi Island [McLaughlin's Island]

Point Carter

Point Carter

Point Migley

Point Whitehorn

Rosario Strait [Ringgold's Channel]

Sandy Point

Semiahmoo [Tongue Point]

Village Point

Viti Rocks

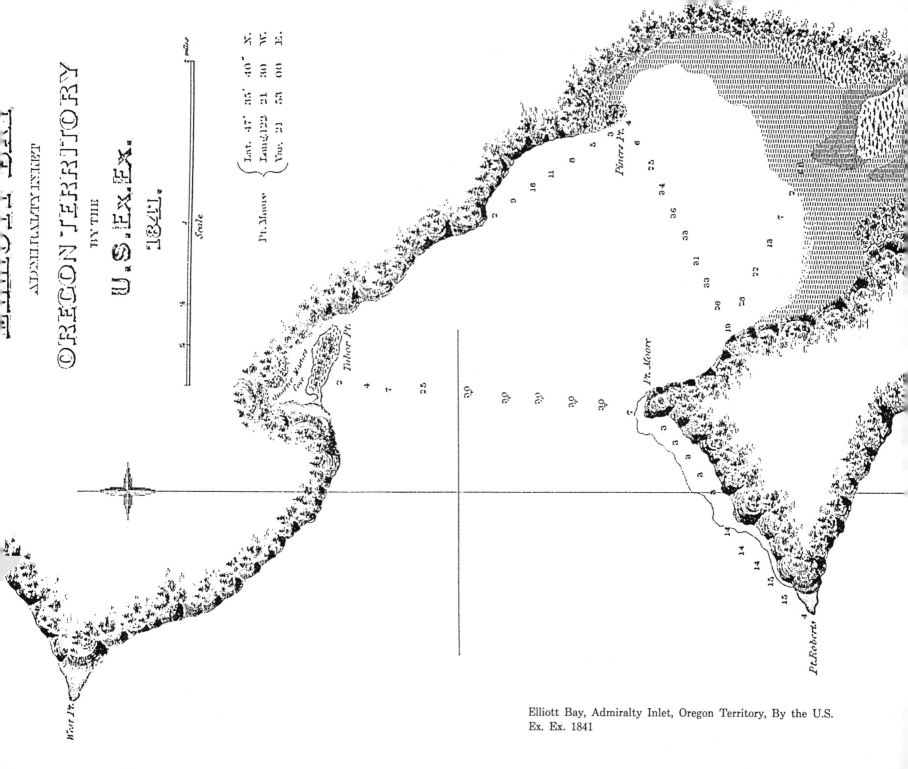

Elliott Bay, Admiralty Inlet, Oregon Territory, By the U.S. Ex. Ex. 1841

APPENDIX

PREFACE

1. *The Hidden Coasts*, by Daniel Henderson. New York, William Sloane Associates, 1953.

2. *The Wilkes Expedition*, by David Tyler. Philadelphia, American Philosophical Society, 1968

CHARLES WILKES - LIEUTENANT COMMODORE

1. This was not the only time Wilkes assumed a rank to which he had not yet been promoted. During the Civil War, Wilkes was promoted to the rank of Commodore and held only an acting appointment as a Rear Admiral. Nonetheless, he signed official communications as Rear Admiral. He similarly elevated the ranks of his junior officers. The Secretary of the Navy, Gideon Welles, wrote Wilkes that "Care should be taken in all official communications signed by yourself or addressed by you to your officers, that the official titles recognized by the Department, and no other, be used." *The Hidden Coasts*, by Daniel Henderson. New York, William Sloane Associates, 1953

2. "Diary of Wilkes in the Northwest," edited by Edmond S. Meany. *Washington Historical Quarterly*, January, 1925, volume 16, number 1; April, 1925, volume 16, number 2; July, 1925, volume 16, number 3; October, 1925, volume 16, number 4; January, 1926, volume 17, number 1; April, 1926, volume 17, number 2; July, 1926, volume 17, number 3.

3. "Diary of Wilkes in the Northwest"

4. "Diary of Wilkes in the Northwest"

5. *The Wilkes Expedition*

6. *The Confederate Navy*, by Philip Van Doren Stern. Bonanza, 1962

7. Civil War Secretary of the Navy Gideon Welles wrote about Wilkes in his diary:
"I have had to write to Wilkes pretty decisively. He is very exacting towards others, but is not himself as obedient as he should be. Interposes his authority to interrupt the execution of the orders of the Department. Wrote him this was not permissible, that I expected his command to obey him, and it was no less imperative that he should obey the orders of the Department."
The Hidden Coasts

THE LURE OF THE PACIFIC, THE CONTEST OF NATIONS

1. Richard Hakluyt (1552? - 1616) was an English geographer whose books chronicled the voyages and discoveries of English explorers. Purchas included de Fuca's story in his 1625 re-issue of Hakluyt's work, *Hakluytus Posthumus*.

2. *Who The Hell Was San Juan: Examining The Names Of San Juan Islands Place Names*, by Doug Cardle. Lopez Island, Washington, Coastal Press, 1982

3. The results of the voyage were suppressed for three-quarters of a century, as Malaspina and Revilla Gigedo both fell into disfavor with the Spanish Prime Minister, Godoy.

4. Cook named this archipelago for the fourth Earl of Sandwich for his patron and First Lord of the Admiralty. The first Earl had been a patron of Samuel Pepys, the premier administrator of the Stuart Navy. The fourth Earl was no less adept at maritime management, and had besides invented the snack which bears his name.

5. *A Voyage to the Pacific Ocean*, by James Cook and James King (London, 1784), as noted in *First Approaches to the Northwest Coast*, by David Pethick. North Vancouver, B. C., Douglas & McIntyre, 1976

6. The search party under d'Entrecasteaux was composed of both royalists and republicans. It was underway at the time of Louis XVI's death at the guillotine in 1793, and on the eve of his death, Louis is reported to have asked "at least, do we have news of Monsieur La Perouse?" *The Last Voyage of La Perouse*, by Robin Inglis. Vancouver, B. C., Vancouver Maritime Museum, 1986

7. *First Approaches to the Northwest Coast*

8. Kellett later engaged in his own Northwest Passage adventure, joining the search for Sir John Franklin's lost Arctic expedition.

9. *First Approaches to the Northwest Coast*

10. *First Approaches to the Northwest Coast*

11. Captain Tipping and the *Sea Otter* vanished without a trace that same year.

12. *First Approaches to the Northwest Coast*

13. The *Beaver* sailed to the Northwest coast in 1835 rigged as a brigantine with its paddle wheels shipped and stored below.

14. *Company of Adventurers*, by Peter C. Newman. Markham, Ontario, Viking, 1985

15. *Company of Adventurers*

16. They noted a number of Indian settlements along the Black and the "Chickelees" (Chehalis) rivers, which they referred to as of the "Holloweena" tribe. This appellation evoked a smile from a former Skokomish tribal council chairman when asked if he had encountered the name in his research. After a pause he asked, "Did these guys come through in October?"

17. John Quincy Adams, at the time President Monroe's Secretary of State, was the author of the agreement.

18. *The Wilkes Expedition*, by David B. Tyler. Philadelphia, American Philosophical Society, 1968

19. *Magnificent Voyagers*, Viola, Herman J., and Carolyn Margolis, editors. Washington, D.C., Smithsonian Institution, 1985

20. The *Peacock* was found to be poorly refitted with a wet gun deck from badly-fitted gun ports. *The Wilkes Expedition*

21. *Puget's Sound: A Narrative of Early Tacoma and the Southern Sound*, by Murray Morgan. Seattle, University of Washington Press, 1979

22. Ironically, for the purposes of this narrative, Wilkes and the 4th Earl of Sandwich were early friends (as members of the "Hellfire Club," or Mendenhall Monks). Later, the two became enemies as Wilkes, opposed to the King's policies, attacked Sandwich as a member of the government (Sandwich, Admiralty First Lord and Cook's patron, played a significant though indirect role in the early Northwest). So exasperated was Sandwich with Wilkes' attacks that, in Parliament, he expostulated, "Damme Sir, I know not whether you'll die of hanging or the pox!" "That depends, My Lord," Wilkes replied, "Upon whether I embrace your principles or your mistress."

23. *The Wilkes Expedition*

24. D'Urville's ship was named in honor of De La Perouse's flagship.

25. "Wilkes' and D'Urville's Discoveries in Wilkes Land," by Rear Admiral J. E. Pillsbury, USN. *United States Naval Institute Proceedings*, June, 1910

26. *Early Maritime Artists of the Pacific Northwest Coast 1741-1841*, by John Henry Frazier. Seattle, University of Washington Press, 1984

27. "Diary of Wilkes in the Northwest," edited by Edmond S. Meany. *Washington Historical Quarterly*, volume 16, number 1, January, 1925; volume 16, number 2, April, 1925; volume 16, number 3, July, 1925; volume 16, number 4, October, 1925; volume 17, number 1, January, 1926; volume 17, number 2, April, 1926; volume 17, number 3, July, 1926

28. Reynold's journal, quoted in *The Wilkes Expedition in Puget Sound 1841*, by Patrick Haskett. Olympia, Washington, State Capitol Museum and Western Interstate Commission on Higher Education, 1974

29. "The Wilkes Exploring Expedition," by Louis Feipel. *U.S. Naval Institute Proceedings*, September, 1914

30. "The Wilkes Exploring Expedition," by Captain G. S. Bryan, USN. *United States Naval Institute Proceedings*, October, 1939

31. *The American Sailing Navy*, by Howard Chappelle. New York, Bonanza, 1949

32. *Connections*, by James Burke. Boston, Little, Brown, 1978

33. "Diary of Wilkes in the Northwest"

"THOUGH FAR FROM OUR HOMES, YET STILL IN OUR LAND"

1. - 6. *Narrative of the United States Exploring Expedition. During the Years 1838, 1839, 1840, 1841, 1842*, by Charles Wilkes. Philadelphia, Lea and Blanchard, 1845

7. "Diary of Wilkes in the Northwest," edited by Edmond S. Meany. *Washington Historical Quarterly*, January, 1925, volume 16, number 1; April, 1925, volume 16, number 2; July, 1925, volume 16, number 3; October, 1925, volume 16, number 4; January, 1926, volume 17, number 1; April, 1926, volume 17, number 2; July, 1926, volume 17, number 3.

8. *Narrative*

9. - 12. "Diary of Wilkes in the Northwest"

13. The observatory was located west of Fort Nisqually, near the present-day town of Du Pont.

14. *Narrative*

15. - 16. "Diary of Wilkes in the Northwest"

17. Wilkes also exhibited a lack of understanding of and empathy with his own crew men and officers. In his diary, he rarely mentions any officer by name, and then usually to list only his shortcomings. Even when the work was done well, Wilkes did not lavish praise on his subordinates. This is in great contrast to explorers such as Vancouver, who frequently gave credit to the work done by others. Moreover, Wilkes rarely referred to common sailors, except as "Jack."

18. *Narrative*

19. "Diary of Wilkes in the Northwest"

20. In 1845, an expedition to find the Northwest Passage, commanded by Sir John Franklin, came to grief in the Arctic. All 129 men on the voyage were lost to scurvy and starvation, and more than 40 rescue missions attempted to find survivors. One reason often cited for this celebrated disaster was the refusal of the expedition's leaders to adopt any of the survival tactics used by the resident Eskimos.

"As viewed from our time, we have in this retreat an appalling case of failure to adapt oneself to conditions. For two years the expedition had been in close touch with Eskimos who were living by seal-hunting, but it does not appear that any of the Europeans learned how to hunt seals, nor, indeed, that they learned any of the elements of northern self-preservation. Instead of seeking big game of the region, they carried fowling pieces and shot birds."

Great Adventures and Explorations, by Vilhjalmur Stefansson. New York, Dial Press, 1947

In the annals of exploration and settlement, this tragic scenario was repeated many times.

21. - 32. "Diary of Wilkes in the Northwest"

33. Wilkes again served as a consultant on the Northwest when he was approached in 1850 by Samuel Royal Thurston, the first territorial delegate to Congress from the Oregon Territory. Thurston was looking for information on good post office locations. *Thurston's Washington City Journal*, as noted by Art Dwelly, publisher of the *Tenino Independent*.

34. *Narrative*

35. Quoted in *The Wilkes Expedition in Puget Sound 1841*, by Patrick Haskett. Olympia, Washington, Washington State Capitol Museum and Western Interstate Commission on Higher Education, 1974

36. - 48. "Diary of Wilkes in the Northwest"

"A STATE THAT IS DESTINED TO CONTROL THE DESTINIES OF THE PACIFIC"

1. *Narrative of the United States Exploring Expedition. During the Years 1838, 1839, 1840, 1841, 1842,* by Charles Wilkes. Philadelphia, Lea and Blanchard, 1845

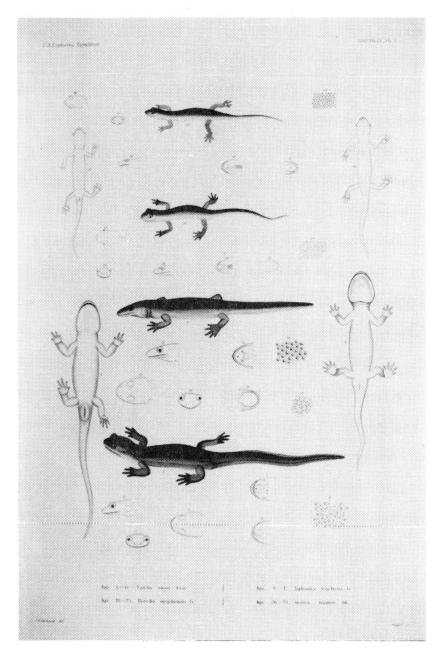

Plate I Atlas to Volume XX
Herpetology
Washington State Library

Plate 15, Atlas to Volume XX, *Herpetology* (Washington State
Library)

BIBLIOGRAPHY

Baird, S. F., Superintendent
Atlas to Volume XX. Herpetology. United States Exploring Expedition. During the Years 1838, 1839, 1840, 1841, 1842. Under the Command of Charles Wilkes, USN Philadelphia, C. Sherman and Son, 1858

Bradford, Gershom
The Mariner's Dictionary
New York, Weathervane Books, 1952

Bryan, Captain G. S.
"The Wilkes Exploring Expedition"
United States Naval Institute Proceedings
October, 1939

Burke, James
Connections
Boston, Little, Brown, 1978

Cardle, Doug
Who the Hell Was San Juan? Examining the Roots of San Juan Islands Place Names
Lopez Island, WA, Coastal Press, 1982

Cassin, John
Atlas to Volume VIII. Mammology and Ornithology. United States Exploring Expedition. During the Years 1838, 1839, 1840, 1841, 1842. Under the Command of Charles Wilkes, USN
Philadelphia, J. B. Lippincott & Co., 1858

Chappelle, Howard
The American Sailing Navy
New York, Bonanza, 1949

Feipel, Louis
"The Wilkes Exploring Expedition"
United States Naval Institute Proceedings
September, 1914

Gould, Augustus A.
Atlas to Volume XII. Mollusca and Shells. United States Exploring Expedition. During the Years 1838, 1839, 1840, 1841, 1842. Under the Command of Charles Wilkes, USN.
Philadelphia, C. Sherman and Son, 1856

Haskett, Patrick
The Wilkes Expedition in Puget Sound 1841
Olympia, Washington, Washington State Capitol Museum and Western Interstate Commission on Higher Education, 1974

Henderson, Daniel
The Hidden Coasts
New York, William Sloane Associates, 1953

Hitchman, Robert
Place Names of Washington
Tacoma, Washington State Historical Society, 1985

Meany, Edmond S.
"Diary of Wilkes in the Northwest"
Washington Historical Quarterly
January, 1925, volume 16, number 1; April, 1925, volume 16, number 2; July, 1925, volume 16, number 3, October, 1925, volume 16, number 4; January, 1926, volume 17, number 1; April, 1926, volume 17, number 2; July, 1926, volume 17, number 3

Meany, Edmond S.
History of the State of Washington
New York, Macmillan Company, 1924

Meany, Edmond S.
Origin of Washington Geographic Names
Detroit, Gale Research Company, 1968

Meany, Edmond S.
Vancouver's Discovery of Puget Sound
Portland, Oregon, Binfords and Mort, 1942

Morgan, Murray
Puget's Sound: A Narrative of Early Tacoma and the Southern Sound
Seattle, University of Washington Press, 1979

Newman, Peter C.
Company of Adventurers
Markham, Ontario, Penguin Books Canada Ltd., 1985

Pethick, Derek
First Approaches to the Northwest Coast
Seattle, University of Washington Press, 1976

Pillsbury, J. E.
"Wilkes' and D'Urville's Discoveries in Wilkes Land"
United States Naval Institute Proceedings
June, 1910

Reed, Rowena
Combined Operations in the Civil War
Annapolis, Naval Institute Press, 1978

Shingleton, Royce
John Taylor Wood, Sea Ghost of the Confederacy
Athens, GA, University of Georgia Press, 1979

Stanton, William
The Great United States Exploring Expedition of 1838-1842
Berkeley, California, University of California Press, 1975

Stefansson, Vilhjalmur
Great Adventures and Explorations
New York, Dial Press, 1947

Stern, Philip Van Doren
The Confederate Navy
New York, Bonanza, 1962

Tyler, David A.
The Wilkes Expedition
Philadelphia, American Philosophical Society, 1968

Viola, Herman J., and Carolyn Margolis, editors
Magnificent Voyagers
Washington, D. C., Smithsonian Institution, 1985

The Visual Encyclopedia of Nautical Terms Under Sail
New York, Crown Publishers, 1978

Wilkes, Charles
Narrative of the United States Exploring Expedition. During the Years 1838, 1839, 1840, 1841, 1842
Philadelphia, Lea and Blanchard, 1845